— *Pr* *se f*

SPINACH IN
YOUR BOSS'S TEETH

Essential Etiquette for Professional Success

Spinach in Your Boss's Teeth: Essential Etiquette for Professional Success, addresses the many facets of business etiquette in an entertaining, no-nonsense way—everything from digital diplomacy to global greetings. It is a must-read for those who want to avoid embarrassment and enhance their professionalism.

—**John Oppenheimer,** CEO of Columbia Hospitality

As a sales expert, I know that successful sales is about connecting with people and presenting your best self. *Spinach in Your Boss's Teeth* covers how to do this and more, whether you're in sales or any other area of business. Arden shares invaluable etiquette and manners information in a warm and easygoing style, extended pinky finger not required. I highly recommend her book to anyone who wants greater professional success.

—**Andrea Sittig-Rolf,** Founder of BlitzMasters and author of *Business-to-Business Prospecting: Innovative Techniques to Get Your Foot in the Door with any Prospect, The Seven Keys to Effective Business-to-Business Appointment Setting,* and *Power Referrals: The Ambassador Method for Empowering Others to Promote Your Business and Do the Selling for You*

Spinach in Your Boss's Teeth demystifies the art and science of business etiquette with practical and insightful advice to gracefully maneuver the most vexing situation.

—**Benson Porter**, President and CEO of BECU

I'm delighted that Arden has written this book. It contains all of the essentials and is a great refresher, even if your interpersonal skills are well-honed. Good people skills can take your business from average or good to outstanding. I recommend that you get Arden's book—it will absolutely help you to be a gracious professional.

—**Bill Nolan,** CEO of Buildingi

Whether you're tweeting for your company, meeting with a client or interviewing over lunch, *Spinach in Your Boss's Teeth* will help professionals navigate the modern workplace with poise and grace. Arden shares concrete advice that is essential for workplace success. This book will help you take your career to the next level.

—**Shari Storm,** CEO of Category 6 Consulting and author of *Motherhood Is the New MBA: Using Your Parenting Skills to Be a Better Boss*

It's a changing world, but one thing that hasn't changed is the importance of treating others with courtesy and respect. Arden Clise imparts her wisdom on how to do just that, while also teaching you how to handle common etiquette dilemmas. Her book is a must-read for anyone who wants to reliably build strong and successful relationships with customers, colleagues … or anyone.

—**John Meisenbach,** Founder and Chairman of MCM

In this increasingly busy, digital world, how you conduct yourself and treat others can make or break your career. This much-needed guide for the modern professional is chock-full of useful and current information that will help anyone make great impressions on others. You'll want to read this book to stay current with today's rules of conduct or to refer to for those sticky situations such as spinach in your boss's teeth!

—**Dr. Julie Miller,** author of *Business Writing That Counts!* and *Secrets of Self-Starters*

After hiring Arden to train our management team, some of my team members have continued to comment that it was the most valuable training they have ever received. And fun, too! She even gave us permission to eat asparagus with our fingers and still remain within correct business etiquette guidelines. So you just have to ask yourself, "Could there be a more enjoyable business lunch?" Read her useful and engaging book to find out. I look forward to using it as a training resource for my staff.

—**Sam Johnson,** General Manager of Pan Pacific Hotel Seattle

As a global career expert and 30-year corporate ladder-climber, I have both witnessed and made career-limiting etiquette errors. I wish I had Ms. Clise's new book, *Spinach in Your Boss's Teeth*, back then! The stories are both interesting and relatable. This book should be required reading for college graduates and on the business bookshelf for all managers and executives. I'm going to share it with all my career- and job-search clients, too.

—**Dana Manciagli**, Global Career Coach and author of *Cut the Crap, Get a Job*

The matter of business etiquette hasn't gotten the attention it deserves in recent years, and Arden Clise is here to remind us that there are distinctive habits that help make a career—and a life—more graceful and more successful.

Arden's approach to the topic is relatable and not the least bit stuffy. The things you learn from her give you confidence and will help set you apart from the crowd. Yes, it does matter where you put the dessert fork, and it does matter on which side you affix your name tag! I am so pleased that Arden put her practical wisdom into this much-needed book.

—**Jim Hessler**, Founder of Path Forward Leadership and co-host of *The Boss Show*

Arden Clise's writing and advice on everyday etiquette is sound, easy to read, practical, and offered with a sense of humor that makes it enjoyable and lighthearted, yet still powerfully effective. Arden doesn't write about the Queen's etiquette, but rather she addresses common etiquette dilemmas that one would encounter in the workplace and socially. Her book is full of answers to frequently asked questions about etiquette that will help the reader feel more comfortable and confident in a variety of situations. Embracing her tips and employing her strategies will help you present your best self and feel great about it at all times. Highly regarded and highly recommended!

—**Debbie Rosemont**, CPO® Productivity Consultant and Trainer, Simply Placed; author of *Six Word Lessons to Be More Productive*

SPINACH IN YOUR BOSS'S TEETH

Essential Etiquette for Professional Success

Arden Clise

SPINACH IN YOUR BOSS'S TEETH
Essential Etiquette for Professional Success

Silver Fern Publishing
6837 29th Avenue Northeast
Seattle, WA 98115 USA
www.silverfernpublishing.com

Cover design by Damonza.com
Interior page design by Lanphear Design
Illustrations by Kelly Roper
Author photo by Shelly Oberman Photography

Clise, Arden.
Spinach in Your Boss's Teeth: Essential Etiquette for Professional Success
Print ISBN: 978-0-9961553-2-8
E-book ISBN: 978-0-9961553-3-5
Library of Congress Control Number: 2016931396

1. Business Etiquette 2. Self-help

Printed in the United States of America

DEDICATION

To my gracious grandmother, Eunice Clise, for giving me my first etiquette book and kindling my love for the subject. She had perfect etiquette. But more importantly, she was one of the kindest, most courteous people I have had the pleasure of knowing.

And to my father, John Clise, who taught me some of my earliest etiquette lessons, and that to be a great conversationalist you need to be a great listener.

CONTENTS

FOREWORD

Maybe you've been to business or social dinners where everyone seated at the table was surreptitiously glancing at the place settings, trying to remember which side their water glass and bread plate should be on. This happened recently when I was at a dinner to honor a major sports star. It appeared that no one wanted to be first to take a sip of water, lest they commit a faux pas.

Fortunately, I was able to tactfully be of assistance. "I recently read something fun and useful in a new book," I said. "It suggested two great ways to remember that your bread plate is on the left, and your water glass is on the right. Bring the thumb and forefinger of your left hand together, with your other fingers extended, and that will make a 'b'—for bread. Bring the thumb and forefinger of your right hand together, and that will make a 'd'—for drink. Or, use 'BMW,' for Bread on the left, Meal in the middle, Water on the right."

"That is terrific—now I'll always be able to remember," the woman on my left said, as she picked up her water glass.

Helpful and memorable tips such as the BMW acronym are a hallmark of *Spinach in Your Boss's Teeth: Essential Etiquette for Professional Success*. Etiquette expert Arden Clise provides invaluable information for anyone who wants to make a good impression, whether networking at a business function, communicating online, talking with clients (with or without spinach in their teeth), or working with colleagues.

In today's complex world, good manners—how we treat each other—are more important than ever to our success. Knowing how to graciously interact with other people enhances relationships, cooperation and productivity, not to mention increasing the positive energy in the world. It even makes us feel good about ourselves.

Like me, you probably had a mentor—a mother, auntie or teacher—who valued good manners and taught you the basics. But today's demands require that you know much more than saying "please" and "thank you," and placing your napkin in your lap, and not talking with food in your mouth. Each of us needs to be thoughtful about how we present ourselves—how we present our brand, to use a current buzzword.

The way we navigate social situations reflects our personal style. It affects how clients and colleagues perceive us, react to us and feel about us, and about the company or organization we represent.

As I pondered how broad the scope of good etiquette really is, I recalled a flight I took as a young mother with a three-year-old. A family emergency meant we had to catch the first available flight from Seattle to San Francisco on a carrier we had not flown before. As I struggled to get my child safely into her seat and to place the carry-on bag in the overhead, a frowning flight attendant curtly demanded, "Shove the bag in the overhead, or I'll take it off the plane." You can imagine how I felt about ever flying that airline again.

For our return trip, I was able to book a flight on our trusted hometown carrier, Alaska Airlines. The flight attendant welcomed us with a warm smile and asked what she could do to make the flight with my preschooler easier. Such a remarkable difference.

Brand loyalty—whether that brand is you personally, or someone you are representing—is often won with the simplest courtesies, consistently extended. That holds true for every communication: with employers, clients, associates and friends.

Image-related self-help books and articles proliferate, with information about wardrobe upgrades, new diets and the latest workouts, but there is less guidance about manners. Being well-groomed, knowledgeable and skilled is beneficial. But for someone to be truly effective, their manners—their behavior—must also be exceptional. When I am deciding between two equally qualified candidates for a position at my company, I always choose the kind and courteous one.

A warm and positive attitude may come naturally, but we can all up our game when it comes to manners. I work in the magazine business, so I have organized annual Magazine Days in Seattle, bringing in publishers and editors of publications to speak such as *GQ, National Geographic, Wired, Sunset* and *Parenting*. It was a coup when John F. Kennedy Jr., founder of *George* magazine, accepted my invitation. He was the guest of honor at our event's formal dinner and was seated to my right, as protocol dictated, since I was hosting the meal.

I was intrigued to learn JFK Jr.'s personal story, which he jumped right into sharing as soon as we were seated. After a few minutes of listening to his fascinating tale, I was tapped on the arm by a colleague seated on my other side. He leaned in and whispered, "We are all hungry. You are the hostess, and everyone is waiting until you pick up your fork."

Oops! Awkward. Fortunately, a prompt from a savvy friend reminded me of my hostess manners.

Arden's book will help you remember things you already knew and will cover many things you didn't know about manners that can make a difference and help you to present yourself in the best light.

Arden, who is also in high demand on the business-speaking circuit, shares her extensive knowledge in this quick-read, user-friendly book. Her writing style, like her personal style, is light and graceful, and exemplifies the wise, well-mannered friend many of us wish we had.

Her book is filled with smart advice for every one of us—from top executives to people at all levels who want to advance in their careers, to business and leisure travelers who want their trips to go well.

It's true: You get only one chance to make a great first impression. The wisdom Arden shares will help you ensure that your first and subsequent interactions reflect favorably on you, indicate your respect for others, and enhance your personal and professional success.

Mimi K. Kirsch
President/Publisher
Paradigm Communications Group

INTRODUCTION

Have you ever wondered what to say to your boss with spinach in her teeth, or which bread plate to use at a crowded table? Maybe you're not sure how to introduce someone whose name you have forgotten. Perhaps you've struggled with how to gracefully exit a conversation at a networking event.

Etiquette dilemmas, even small ones, can trip us up and make us feel uncomfortable and less confident. And when we feel unsure, we can't be our best selves. If the business meal with the important prospective client is focused more on navigating the place setting than on making a positive connection, you risk losing the deal. Or if you continually forget someone's name, that person may feel unimportant to you, and that can affect your relationship.

Being knowledgeable about etiquette makes navigating the world easier. And, lest you think etiquette is about knowing how to drink tea in fancy cups, pinky out, while eating pink-frosted cakes, you'll be happy to hear it is nothing of the sort. Etiquette is not about being perfect and uptight. It simply defines the rules and guidelines that help you know how to handle social and professional situations. When you know what to do, you can relax.

When I was a child, it seemed my parents were always correcting my manners. I thought all the fuss was silly and unimportant. I especially disliked learning how to hold my eating utensils properly. But years later, when I was faced with my first business meal and I knew what to do with the array of silverware, plates and glasses on the table (while those around me looked panicked), I realized that what I'd learned as a child had value. I could relax at these events because I wasn't worried about which bread plate to use, or what to do with my napkin.

However, knowing how to gracefully end a conversation or even how to make a proper business introduction was a different matter. This wasn't something I'd learned, so I felt tripped up by those and other situations until I learned from mentors, books and etiquette school. The more I've studied etiquette, the more confident and comfortable I have become. I'm not perfect; I still make mistakes. And I'm learning every day.

I've also discovered that good etiquette—or the lack of it—can affect your career, your income and your life. Seemingly small etiquette faux pas such as sending an email with text speak or talking too loudly in your cubicle can have negative ramifications for your career.

People usually won't tell you if you have poor etiquette, and they probably shouldn't unless that person is a boss or mentor. However, there are numerous examples, many of them in this book, about people who lacked etiquette knowledge and were fired from jobs, missed out on promotions, failed at job interviews or lost clients. Practicing good etiquette will help you be more successful in your profession.

Etiquette has evolved over the centuries to adjust to our changing world. You would find no mention in an etiquette book from the early nineteenth century about smartphones, email, women in the workplace or the do's and don'ts for airplane travel. But today, etiquette rules do address those topics.

ETIQUETTE VERSUS MANNERS

The one constant in etiquette books dating as far back as the sixteenth century is the importance of kindness, respect and courtesy. Dutch thinker and author Erasmus wrote in his book *On Civility of Children*, "Be lenient toward the offenses of others. A companion ought to not be less dear to you because he has worse manners. There are people who make up for the awkwardness of their behavior by other gifts. If one of your comrades unknowingly gives offense, tell him so alone and say it kindly."[1]

Erasmus was talking about manners and civility, which is different from etiquette. You might say manners are a sister to etiquette.

I've heard it said that etiquette means knowing which fork to use, manners is not saying anything when your neighbor doesn't. My friend Beth Buelow, founder of The Introvert Entrepreneur, a company that provides coaching and consulting for introverted business owners, wisely put it this way, "Etiquette helps *you* be more comfortable and manners make *others* more comfortable." Both manners and etiquette are important for social and professional success. This book will address mostly business etiquette, and will include some manners guidelines as well.

HOW YOU'LL BENEFIT FROM READING THIS BOOK

I hope this book will help you to be more confident and poised as you navigate the business world, which ultimately will lead to your professional success. Whether you are new to the workplace or are a seasoned executive, you will find helpful information on everything from how to make great first and lasting impressions, to how to conduct productive business meetings, master social media do's and don'ts and mingle with ease.

Some of what you read may seem like common sense. But ask yourself, am I practicing these "common" tenets? It's easy to assume we are being mannerly and others aren't. As you read this book, follow the advice that is helpful to you and that applies to your industry. If you find yourself pushing back on the recommendations, ask yourself why. Is it because it doesn't relate to you, or is it because you realize you might have to make some changes in how you're presenting yourself or how you're interacting with others? You are free to ignore the advice, but be aware that your decision could negatively affect your job or career.

Oh, and that question about spinach in a boss's teeth? Discreetly say something to the unaware soul to help her avoid further embarrassment from having the abject object displayed for all to see throughout the day. I'll answer the other questions throughout the book.

CHAPTER ONE

HANDSHAKE OR FIST BUMP?

Presenting Your Best Self

A client wanted her employees to make a good impression on visitors at an expo booth they were staffing for the first time. Through training, the employees learned to engage and respectfully greet booth visitors, demonstrate professionalism through their body language, and build rapport to gain leads and clients. Once at the trade show, the employees practiced open and welcoming body language and communication. Their booth was very busy with visitors while the booths on either side had very little traffic. My client was thrilled that they came home with several qualified leads and a couple of new clients, which she attributed to how the employees presented themselves.

Think for a moment of someone who made a great first impression on you. What did you notice? What did you hear?

When I go over this exercise with my clients, I often hear comments such as: the person was dressed well, she appeared confident through good posture, he had a firm handshake and steady eye contact, or she smiled and was well-spoken. On the phone, someone who was impressive had a warm tone and vocal variety; the words he used conveyed confidence and he had few if any audible pauses such as "um" and "uh."

Now think of someone who didn't impress you. Perhaps this person slouched in her chair, or had a weak handshake. Maybe this colleague regularly swore or dressed as if he was headed to the gym rather than to work. Did his behavior or appearance affect what you thought of him?

How we present ourselves—from our body language, eye contact, attire and communication—is an important aspect of etiquette and can have an impact on our career. To make a great first and lasting impression, we need to pay attention to all of these elements.

BODY LANGUAGE

Your body communicates your mental and emotional state, yet often we aren't aware of the messages it conveys. For instance, sometimes to my consternation, my face will communicate my feelings before I've verbalized them. I would probably make a terrible gambler. But knowing my face can be more communicative than I desire means I pay more attention to my expressions in stressful situations. I can consciously adopt a more relaxed or passive face. I'll cover more on how to do this later in the chapter.

Let's look at the five aspects of body language—eye contact, posture, body movement, gestures and facial expressions—and how they affect the way people perceive you. I've included some relatively easy actions you can take that will communicate confidence and friendliness.

Eye Contact

In the United States and most Western cultures, eye contact communicates self-assurance and respect. Have you ever had a conversation with someone who didn't look at you throughout the encounter? How did you feel about this person? I would imagine you either felt he was uninterested in what you were saying or you doubted his self-confidence.

Look into someone's eyes when you meet and when you are conversing. However, be careful not to stare, which can be uncomfortable for others and can be seen as threatening. Hold a steady gaze about 60 to 70 percent of the time. When you're not looking at the other person, avoid looking down or darting your eyes to avoid eye contact.

When speaking to a group, look equally at each person. Hold eye contact with one person for a few seconds or long enough to say a sentence or phrase. This helps you to make a genuine connection and keeps you from looking and feeling nervous.

Posture

A slumped posture shows a lack of self-esteem and confidence. Someone who has good posture appears more self-assured. Stand or sit up straight, as if the top of your head is being pulled up by a string. Pull your shoulders back and hold your head level to the ground over your shoulders. Stand evenly on both feet, which should be directly under your shoulders. Avoid the nervous gesture of shifting back and forth between your feet. And never slouch when sitting in a chair. Sit up straight and be present. You'll exude more professionalism.

Body Movement

When moving about, whether walking into the office or making your way to a meeting, keep these points in mind:

- Move with fluidity and unhurried energy. Have a neutral walking pace that's not too fast or too slow. When you walk hurriedly, you can appear as if you don't have things under control. If you manage a staff, they will be especially aware of how fast you're walking. If you're dashing about, they will wonder if something is wrong.

- Keep your strides even and slightly long as opposed to short, quick or uneven strides. Let your arms swing naturally but not excessively.

Gestures

Gestures include movement of our hands, face and sometimes other parts of the body. Gestures can be intentional or unconscious.

Let's start with a few gestures to avoid:

- Crossing your arms, which can make you seem defensive, afraid or judgmental.

- Pulling on your shirt collar, rubbing your arms or forehead, or using other pacifying gestures, which can signal you are uncomfortable or insecure.

- Rubbing your nose, covering your mouth or tugging at your ear, which are all signs you are anxious or unsure of yourself.

- Crossing your leg across your other leg, which can seem too casual. Keep your feet on the floor or crossed at the ankles.

- Flailing or flip-flopping your hands when you speak. Use your hands moderately and purposefully.

To avoid looking disengaged or defensive, don't lean back when talking to others. To show interest, lean in toward the person or people in the meeting.

A colleague interviewed for a CEO position and did not get the job. I heard that one of the negative things the interviewers noted about him was that he leaned back during the interview. They thought he appeared arrogant because of this. It's amazing how even a little thing like leaning back can have such a big impact on how you are perceived.

Try to avoid fidgeting, such as playing with a pen, clasping and unclasping your hands, moving around in your chair or playing with your jewelry or hair. All of those movements communicate nervousness. If you have a tendency to fidget, put your hands in your lap or on the table and leave them there.

Think of someone who is always poised and put together. She doesn't rush, she doesn't seem harried or anxious, and her gestures and movement always seem under control. This is the image you want to convey.

Handshakes. Shaking hands is not exactly a gesture, but your handshake falls under body language because it communicates so much. In most Western cultures, both men and women shake hands in business when they meet, greet, say goodbye or seal the deal. Interestingly, the handshake likely originated in the fifth century BC as a sign of peace. People would shake hands to show they weren't holding a weapon. The up-and-down pump is believed to have started as a way to dislodge a weapon hidden in a person's sleeve!

While we usually don't have to worry about hidden weapons today, the handshake continues to be a way of acknowledging another person. But did you know your handshake talks behind your back? A weak, sweaty or partial handshake will communicate anxiety and a lack of confidence. If it's painfully firm, you may be seen as overly aggressive.

When I discuss handshaking in trainings, I often get quite a bit of discussion and questions because people have such strong opinions about bad handshakes.

A confident handshake occurs when you put your whole hand into the other person's hand so that you are touching web to web—that area between your thumb and your pointer finger. Wrap your fingers around the other person's hand. Your grip should be firm but not bone-crushing. Maintain eye contact throughout the handshake. Pump two to three times and then let go. It can be uncomfortable to others if you hold on longer than three pumps. Also, avoid clasping the person's hand or arm with your left hand. This typical politician or funeral-parlor handshake is meant to communicate warmth and friendliness, but for many people, it can seem insincere, forced or simply too intimate in business situations.

Always stand when you shake hands, unless you are stuck behind a table. In that case, lift up a bit when shaking the other person's hand.

Women and men shake hands the same way, and men do not need to wait for a woman to extend her hand. Either can initiate a handshake. Additionally, women do not need to give a feminine handshake, and men do not need to give a less firm handshake to a woman. However, if the person whose hand you're shaking is elderly or appears to have arthritis, use a softer grip.

Facial Expressions

Your facial expression needs to match what you are saying. Smiling is usually a positive, confident facial expression that can put you and others at ease. However, avoid smiling when you're talking about something serious or sad. Be sure your smile is sincere. A fake smile is one in which only your mouth is lifted, whereas a genuine smile involves the whole face and crinkles your eyes.

Facial expressions and gestures you want to avoid include: wetting your lips, repeated swallowing, excessive throat clearing, a scared or uneasy look on your face and rapid eye blinking. All of these give the signal that you are anxious.

Before a stressful meeting, practice the following tips to relax your face so that you have a more approachable expression.

- Let your face completely relax as if you're watching TV or are reading the paper. Feel your facial muscles release.

- Move your jaw back and forth and up and down a few times.

- Stick your tongue out as far as you can for a few seconds.

ETIQUETTE DILEMMA

Q. *How much room should I give a person when conversing with her?*

A. *In the United States, we are comfortable with two and a half to four feet of space between colleagues or acquaintances. If someone continues to back up when you're talking to her, she is most likely uncomfortable with how close you are standing. Don't follow her. Give her space, as they say.*

- Now think positive, confident thoughts. This will usually lead to a slight smile and warm expression on your face. Don't force it; just let your happy feelings show up on your face.

Specific Body Language Tips for Women

Many women unconsciously try to make themselves small. In business meetings, women often keep their materials close to them, elbows in and legs tightly crossed. To convey confidence, take up space—spread your meeting items out and put your arms on the chair arms or on the table, rather than folded in your lap. Sit up straight and keep your feet on the floor.[1]

To communicate credibility, pay attention to a few body-language specifics:

- Avoid touching your jewelry, twirling your hair or fussing with your clothes. These gestures suggest a lack of maturity and self-confidence.

- Be careful of how often you tilt your head when listening to others. Women tend to do this to show interest or concern. While at times this can be an appropriate gesture, too much head tilting can make you seem submissive or flirtatious. To convey confidence and authority, hold your head level.

- Avoid excessive head nodding. A few head nods are normal and show encouragement to the speaker, but continual head nods give the impression you feel subservient.

The first time I appeared on TV, I was quite nervous. Despite preparing my talking points and being coached by a friend who had been on the same show, my nerves still flared up once I was in the studio. Consequently, I did a lot of head nodding and some head tilting when the host was talking to me. A couple of times, I looked like a bobblehead doll—up down, up down. I was also guilty of flighty flip-flop hands. These were all signs that I was nervous. But seeing them later on video helped me become more aware of these gestures so I could avoid them in other nerve-racking situations.

EFFECTIVE COMMUNICATION

How you speak contributes to the impression you make on others. A friend shared with me her experience looking for a new dentist. She called several different dentists' offices to learn more about their background and fees. She said that

ETIQUETTE DILEMMA

Q. *What should I do with my hands when I'm making a presentation or talking to someone?*

A. *Ah, yes, the "my-hands-are-aliens-and-I-don't-know-what-to-do-with-them" dilemma. Many people have a tendency to hold them in the fig leaf position (in front of your private parts), reverse fig leaf (behind you) or the "hold-onto-the-lectern-for-dear-life" position. The fig leaf looks as if you're protecting yourself from those menacing audience members. Holding your hands behind your back appears as if you're hiding something. And the white-knuckle grip on the lectern will do nothing to assure your audience that you're feeling comfortable. Instead, keep your arms held down loosely by your sides, palms turned slightly out at a 45-degree angle, unless you are making a point. Use your hands moderately between your waist and shoulders to make a point or to illustrate something you're speaking about.[2] This will appear the most natural and confident. It may feel uncomfortable at first, but keep practicing. It will get easier.*

she spoke to one receptionist who didn't know much about the dentist, and her speech was full of audible pauses—um, ah. She also used a lot of slang. While the dentist might have been very accomplished, his receptionist presented herself so unprofessionally that my friend assumed the dentist was not very skilled. She crossed him off her list.

You know that the words you use have an impact on your listeners. But just as important are tone of voice, pace and rhythm, volume, pronunciation and enunciation.

Tone of Voice

Your tone can communicate whether you're asking a question or not. For instance, if your tone goes up at the end of a sentence it makes what you're saying a question. But when you have a rising intonation at the end of a sentence that isn't a question, you can appear unsure of yourself. This is called upspeaking. Australians use this sing-songy way of speaking, which is charming in Australia, but not so much in the United States.

A friend of mine is from Switzerland and speaks fluent French. I studied French for many years in school, but I hadn't spoken it for years. I asked her if we could have a conversation in French.

.... 🍃 ....

ETIQUETTE DILEMMA

Q. *Handshakes are so yesterday. Can I offer a fist bump instead?*

A. *Unless you work for a company that promotes fist bumping for germ reasons, it's not an acceptable greeting in the workplace. Someone will expect a handshake and your balled-up fist will create an awkward moment. Fist bump away with your friends, but not with your colleagues.*

Because I wasn't sure I was using the right words or accent, I kept ending my sentences with a rising intonation. Finally, my friend said to me, "I'm not sure if you're asking me a question or not." My insecurity was coming through in my tone.

The tone of your voice can also express your emotional state. A light, bright tone is usually perceived as friendly and warm, whereas a flat tone or monotone can show boredom or a lack of enthusiasm. A sarcastic or grumpy tone is one to avoid as well.

A client was referred to me because she was irritating her bosses, colleagues and customers. When she was asked to do something, she said the right words, but she used a snippy or caustic tone. The phrase "I'm happy to help you with that" turned into a clear expression of her unhappiness at having to do the task. She was about to lose her job, but through coaching she became aware of the problem and learned how to use a friendlier tone. She was able to consciously turn the situation around. Last I heard, she is still happily employed.

Try to have a warm tone, especially when speaking on the phone when people can't see your body language. You can achieve this simply by smiling. Put a mirror next to your phone so you're reminded to smile when you pick up the handset; the smile will be expressed in your voice.

Avoid speaking in a high-pitched voice, which can sound immature. A lower pitch sounds more confident and professional. To lower your pitch, imagine your voice is "walking" downstairs. As you envision descending the stairs, repeatedly say "ha" while you make your pitch get lower with each step. Find a pitch that is in the medium to lower ranges yet still comfortable for you. Practice speaking at that pitch.

As Margaret Thatcher ascended in her career she worked with a voice coach to help lower her voice. If you feel your high-pitched voice is affecting your credibility, consider working with a vocal coach.

Pace and Rhythm

Pace and rhythm involve the rate at which you speak and your use of pauses. Both affect the meaning, clarity and effectiveness of what you're saying. If you speak too fast, you can seem in a hurry or impatient. Your listeners can have difficulty understanding you, and they can feel rushed. However, if you speak too slowly, you can bore or frustrate your audience.

You should aim for a moderate speaking pace that is about 140 words per minute. In addition, add pauses so it is more interesting to listen to you. This is especially true when you are speaking to an audience. Pauses give your listeners a chance to gather their thoughts and bring their focus back to you.

Volume

The volume of your speech is another aspect of communication. Strive for a volume that is not too loud, (which can communicate aggressiveness), nor too soft (which can make you appear unsure of yourself).

Pronunciation and Enunciation

Your pronunciation and enunciation also matter. I recall a political poll taker who called me before a national election. As she asked me questions about the various candidates and elected officials, she stumbled over most of their names. Because of this, she came across as uninformed.

It's important to pronounce names and words correctly to avoid looking ignorant or uneducated. When in doubt, look up a word in the dictionary for the phonetic spelling or use an online dictionary to hear the word pronounced. Or simply choose a different word.

How you enunciate your words matters too. Have you ever had a conversation with someone who ran his words together—who didn't speak clearly and concisely? You probably had a hard time understanding him. Maybe he even sounded as though he'd been nipping at the bottle. Not a great image to convey. Be careful to enunciate your words so that people can understand what you're saying. Sometimes that means slowing down so that your words don't run together. Don't rush or skip over letters with "hard" sounds, including d, k, t and p, or even soft consonants, like h and r. If you're game, you could put marbles in your mouth and try to speak clearly, like Eliza Doolittle was made to do in *My Fair Lady*. At the very least you'll have a good laugh!

Confident Language

Try to use language that sounds confident and avoid words and phrases that communicate uncertainty. For instance, using phrases such as "most certainly" or "in my experience" will convey confidence in what you are saying. However, phrases like, "Do you know what I mean?" or "I'm not an expert, but..." will make you seem unsure of yourself. Also, adding the word "just" communicates insecurity—as in "I just want to make a point." Jettison "just" and speak with authority.

If you struggle with any of these speech patterns, consider hiring a speech coach or joining Toastmasters International, a professional speaking and leadership organization with clubs in cities and towns all over the world. I joined Toastmasters many years ago and I learned to speak confidently in public. The experience changed my life. I walked in the door with my knees knocking, lips stuck to my teeth and a dread of public speaking. I left as a professional speaker thanks to the regular practice and feedback from my fellow Toastmasters.

Swearing, Slang and More

Think twice before swearing in the workplace. In a CareerBuilder study, 81 percent of employers think an employee who swears is less professional, 71 percent believe an employee who swears lacks self-control and 68 percent feel they lack maturity. Another 54 percent of respondents reported they felt those who swear are less intelligent.[3] Swearing will make you less worthy of promotions.

While a very occasional, deserved and modest curse word used to express your feelings is probably not going to negatively affect your career, a regular potty mouth will. Bite your tongue, or come up with some innocuous, even comical words or phrases you could use instead:

- "Oh cupcakes!"
- "Gosh darn it!"
- "For the love of money!"
- "Dagnabit!"
- And my favorite, "Oh, for crying out loud!"

You get the idea.

Slang is another troublemaker. Watch out for these jargon expressions and avoid them in a professional setting. Start worrying if you say "no worries" or "no problem" in response to "thank you." The problem with "no problem" and "no worries" is that they imply you were not inconvenienced by doing the deed you are being thanked for. It is similar to saying, "Oh, this old thing," when someone compliments you; it pushes the compliment away and doesn't honor the praise. Instead, say "You're welcome" or, even nicer, "My pleasure," both of which respect the person for saying "thank you" and acknowledges her gratitude.

I've also heard a lot of people say "no worries" when someone apologizes for inconveniencing them—for example, "I'm sorry you had to stay late to help me with my computer." Rather than responding, "No worries," say "It wasn't a problem," or "I was happy to help."

Okay, you may be thinking, "I've been saying 'No worries' my whole adult life. To me, it's like the French saying 'de rien' (it's nothing) when someone thanks them." And you're right— depending on the situation, it is acceptable. But definitely don't say "no worries" to a boss or client. The expression may be fine among your friends—especially if your tone is warm and friendly, not dismissive.

Another phrase I encourage you not to use, especially in the professional world, is "you guys," as in "Do you guys want to go out for lunch?" I try hard not to use this phrase because it's informal and can be insulting when addressing women, who certainly aren't guys. Since "you" is both a singular and plural pronoun, there is no need to add "guys" after the word when talking about a group. You can say "you two" or "all of you" to address a group.

....

POWERFUL PHRASES

A few words and phrases that are always well received include: "thank you," "please," "my pleasure" and "you're welcome." These terms are never out of style.

....

Other expressions to avoid include: "you betcha"; "back at you"; "awesome"; "totally"; "like," as in "Like, you know, that's totally awesome"; "just sayin'" etc. Record yourself speaking to a colleague for ten minutes and write down all of the slang words you use. You might be surprised by what unknowingly comes out of your mouth.

GROOMING

First impressions also include your attire and grooming. I know it may seem obvious, but I encourage you to pay attention to these seemingly small details. Be sure your shoes are shined, your hair is clean and combed, your clothes are pressed and your nails are clean and clipped. Women, if you wear nail polish, make sure it isn't chipped. And don't forget the soap and deodorant. But do skip the heavy cologne or perfume. *(See more about this topic in Chapter 2.)*

ETIQUETTE DILEMMA

Q. *What if I don't know how to pronounce someone's name when calling her on the phone?*

A. *Learn a few pronunciation basics. A silent "e" at the end of a name makes the vowel in the middle of the name sound like the letter in the alphabet. For instance, the "i" in my name Clise is pronounced like "nice," rather than like "lease" or "fish." If you still can't figure out the person's name, state it the way you think it should be pronounced and ask, "Did I pronounce your name correctly?"*

JOB INTERVIEWS

Job interviews are one of the most anxiety-provoking first-impression scenarios because so much is at stake. To add to the distress, many people feel uncomfortable promoting themselves. But if you are dressed well, use confident body language and communicate assuredly, you will enjoy more success. Here are some additional ways to be even more impressive in an interview:

Do Your Research

Start by doing your homework. Learn all you can about the company, the job—taking time to really understand the job description—and the people with whom you will interview. This will help you to speak more effectively about the position and to ask appropriate questions. And when you have information about the interviewer(s), you have fodder for small talk, making it easier to build rapport.

Look at the company website to find news releases and company news. The more you know about the company and the person you are to meet, the more impressive you'll be when you ask informed questions.

Dress One Step Up

When you dress a notch above how people typically dress at the company it shows that you're serious about the job and that you are a professional. Most companies follow a business casual dress code, so one step up would usually be business attire. Business attire consists of a suit and tie for men and a pant or skirt suit for women, with understated jewelry. That said, if it's a casual firm, you can lose the suit and tie. Instead, men can wear a dress shirt with or without a jacket and nice slacks. Women can wear a dress, a skirt or dress pants with a high-quality knit or silk blouse under a sweater or jacket. A dress shirt without a jacket would also be appropriate.

Stash the Phone

Silence your cell phone, and don't look at it during the interview. At my last job, a manager interviewed someone who answered his phone three times during the interview and said, "It's important" each time. Needless to say, he didn't get the job.

....

TIMING TIP

The ideal time to arrive at an interview is about ten minutes before the meeting time. Arriving any later than five minutes before the appointment can be construed as being late and it may cost you the job.

....

Be Nice to the Receptionist

When you arrive, greet the receptionist, state your name and tell him who you're meeting. Be friendly, and if he isn't busy, engage him in a short conversation. You could comment on the weather or the office building if it's particularly noteworthy or has a great view. The impression you make on the receptionist is likely to be shared with the hiring manager, so think of him as part of the interview and treat him with respect.

Avoid looking at your phone or slouching while waiting. If the receptionist is occupied, simply sit with good posture and think positive thoughts about the interview.

Confidently Greet the Interviewer

When the interviewer greets you, give her a firm handshake accompanied by a smile and eye contact throughout the handshake.

Once escorted into the interview room, wait to be told where to sit down. If you're not directed where to sit, ask. If you're wearing a jacket, leave it on even if the interviewer is dressed more casually or takes his or her jacket off. If your jacket is buttoned, unbutton it before sitting down.

Responding to Questions

During the interview, you'll most likely be asked about previous jobs and how you felt about them. Never say anything negative about previous employers. Even if the interviewer sounds sympathetic, this will reflect badly on you. Focus only on the positive aspects of former employers.

When asked the question, "Tell us about yourself," this is not the time to share anything and everything about your past: "I grew up in a small house in a small town with five siblings, three gerbils, two dogs and a cat..." Instead speak to the jobs or experiences that apply to the position you're interviewing for. Focus on your professional life and not on your personal life. You also could share some of your strengths. For instance, you could say, "I've been praised by previous employers for being a positive team player who has a strong work ethic."

Keep Your Hands Still

I know interviewing is nerve-racking, but try to avoid looking nervous by fidgeting or playing with your hair, jewelry, a pen or other items. Something that helped me to keep from fidgeting in interviews was to clasp my hands on the table or on my lap.

Interviews over a Meal

If the interview is conducted over a meal be mindful of what you order. Watch out for large sandwiches and shellfish, and stringy foods like spaghetti and mozzarella-laden pizza. It's hard to gracefully eat these challenging foods, and that glob of cheese on your chin sure won't help you get the job. Take small bites so you can chew and swallow quickly to answer questions without a mouth full of food. *(For a list of fail-safe foods for interviews and client meetings, see A Few Foods to Avoid in Chapter 4.)*

When it comes to beverages, you might be tempted to order an alcoholic drink to calm your nerves. But don't, even if the interviewer does. Not only could you potentially say something you wish you hadn't, the interviewer might wonder if you have a drinking problem. If the interviewer orders an alcoholic beverage, request something non-alcoholic, such as iced tea, lemonade or seltzer.

Come with a List of Questions

Since you've done your research, you should have a list of questions about the company, the position, the manager and the hiring process (number of candidates, when they hope to make a decision, etc.). My clients tell me they are always impressed by a candidate who asks well-informed, thoughtful questions. However, be careful not to ask questions about the position which are answered in the job description. A friend said that she has interviewed many otherwise very qualified candidates who do this, which appears as if they didn't fully read the description.

Follow Up

At the end of the interview, be sure to thank the interviewer(s) and state your interest in the job. If the interviewer hasn't already given you her business card, go ahead and ask for it so that you have her contact information. And as she walks you out, make small talk to build rapport. Shake her hand before parting.

And don't forget to send a thank-you note within 24 hours after the interview. A colleague recently wrote an article for a magazine about salary negotiations and interviews. Everyone she interviewed mentioned that only a fraction of the candidates write thank-you notes of any kind (digital or longhand). The people she interviewed said that when they did receive thank-you notes it made a positive impression.

Whether you send a handwritten note or email depends on the company. If it's a high-tech firm, an email expressing your thanks will suffice. However, if the company is more traditional or conservative, send both an email and a handwritten thank-you note. Sending both allows you to get the thanks via email

ETIQUETTE DILEMMA

Q. *Is it acceptable to address someone I meet by his first name?*

A. *It depends on the person, the situation and how the person introduces himself. If the person greets you by your last name (Ms. Smith), then you should address him by his last name as well. But if he says "You must be Jane Smith," go ahead and call him by his first name. If he is much older than you, address him by his last name, as in Mr. Jones. He might ask you to call him by his first name, but if he doesn't, it's safer to be a little more formal with someone who is older and continue to address him by his last name.*

to them right away. Following up with a handwritten note will make you stand out among the candidates.

In your note, include these points:

- Thank the interviewer for inviting you to interview for the job.
- State your interest in the job and the company.
- Write a sentence about what you have to offer the company.
- Sign it "Sincerely," or "Best regards," followed by your name.

If someone helped you get the interview, send him a thank-you note as well. And if you get the job, take him out to lunch or dinner to celebrate! You both deserve it.

You can also send a thank-you note to the hiring manager if you *didn't* get the job. Express your thanks for considering you and ask her to keep you in mind should her needs change in the future. You never know when the company may need someone with your skill set. *(See Thank-you Notes in Chapter 5 for more information about stationery and writing thank-you notes.)*

We don't get a second chance to make a first impression, so make sure you are positively impressing those you meet and interact with. Your professional reputation will benefit from paying attention to these details.

CHAPTER TWO

KETCHUP ON YOUR SHIRT

Dressing to Impress

While I was being interviewed for an article in Real Simple *magazine, the writer shared a story with me about hiring an attorney. She said she was referred to someone who came highly recommended. This lawyer worked for a large, respected law firm and had graduated in the top of her class at a prestigious law school. However, when the two met, the attorney was wearing flip-flops, casual pants and a camisole underneath a flannel shirt. "Needless to say, I took the work elsewhere," the writer told me. She simply did not feel this woman was professional and, therefore, she couldn't trust her to manage her affairs.*

....

Imagine your doctor showing up to an appointment wearing shorts, flip-flops and a t-shirt; or a salesperson arriving at a sales presentation wearing sweats. No doubt, you would question the sanity and good judgment of both of them. Worried they weren't up for the job, you might even choose to see a different doctor or go with the salesperson's competition.

How you dress in the workplace is no different. If you show up wearing jeans and a tank top to an important meeting, people will doubt your professionalism, as in the case of the attorney above.

Clothes serve as more than a way to keep us warm and modest; they are part of our personal and professional brand. They are our uniform, you might say. We have expectations that people will wear attire that fits their profession.

DRESS CODES

There are three dress codes in the workplace: casual, business casual and business attire. Different situations, events and workplaces call for different dress codes. What might be inappropriate in one workplace may be perfectly acceptable in another. When in doubt, it's always best to ask your manager or someone in human resources for attire recommendations. The dress codes listed below are guidelines. They are not meant to be definitive for every person and workplace.

Casual Attire

Let's start with the most casual dress—casual attire—or what's often referred to as Casual Friday attire. Items that fall in this category include:

- Khakis.
- Sometimes jeans, as long as they are dark and without holes or fraying.
- Polo shirts, open-collared shirts, knit shirts, and short-sleeved, button-down shirts.
- A cotton sweater.

Women also have the option of wearing an informal skirt or dress, perhaps made of cotton or a synthetic versus wool. The skirt or dress should be modest, no shorter than two inches above the knee and not too tight. You should be able to "pinch an inch" (at a minimum) of fabric on each side around your hips and thighs. If the skirt or dress rides up when seated and you're frequently tugging it down, reserve it for non-work events.

Now we should talk shoes. Loafers and black or brown casual shoes are appropriate for casual wear. But save the athletic shoes for the weekend unless you work in a very casual office. In some workplaces, women may wear peep-toe and open-toed shoes. Sandals for women are usually acceptable in the summer months. Be sure your feet and toes are sandal-ready—your toenails are short and in good condition, your feet are smooth and, if you're wearing nail polish, it isn't chipped or grown out.

If your company has a summer picnic, appropriate attire would also fall under casual attire, but there is a little more leeway. In addition to the attire listed above, Bermuda or walking shorts for women and men are acceptable, and bare arms are fine. Women will want to avoid wearing anything that is strapless, revealing or body hugging. Both men and women need to nix clothes that are sloppy, ripped or faded, have holes in them, or are too big or too tight. Even though it's a casual affair, it's still business related, so modesty and professionalism are expected.

Business Casual

The next level is business casual, which is one step up from casual attire. While not as formal as suits and ties, it includes elements of them.

Men's business casual attire. For men, business casual calls for dress pants, and sometimes chinos are acceptable. Appropriate shirts are dress shirts, with or without a tie, and could include dressy polo shirts. A man may wear a sport coat or blazer, a sweater vest or sweater over a dress shirt or just the shirt without a jacket. Wear dress shoes that lace and make sure they are polished. Some workplaces allow loafers, which are slip-on shoes. A man's shoes should complement his pants. Dark pants call for dark shoes. If wearing lighter slacks, brown shoes are appropriate.

Women's business casual attire. Women have a wider range of options than men when it comes to business casual attire, and that can make it more confusing. It's a blessing and a curse, isn't it ladies? Appropriate shirts include knit or silk tops, sweater sets, a turtleneck or a dress shirt. If the shirt is sleeveless, wear a sweater or jacket over it to cover your arms when you're meeting with clients or upper management.

You might be wondering, why do bare arms need to be covered up? When you show a lot of skin, the focus becomes more on your body and less on your brain. If you want to be taken seriously, it's best to cover up more than you would when not in the workplace. You don't need to wear a hot wool jacket. If the weather is warm, wear a light sweater over that sleeveless shirt or dress.

As far as pants and skirts go, women can wear dress pants, khaki pants or a professional skirt or dress that's no shorter than two inches above the knee. Dressy capris are sometimes allowed in more casual or creative companies. Wear shoes that have a low to moderate heel no more than three and half inches high. Sandals and slides (backless shoes, also known as mules) are not appropriate in some workplaces. Check with your manager or human resources department if you're not sure.

Business Attire

The next dress level is business attire. It used to be considered de rigueur for professional dress, and it is pretty cut and dried— men wear suits and ties, women wear pant or skirt suits. The jacket and pants match and are purchased together. If your jacket is more of a sports coat or is different from the pants, it is not considered business attire. The cut of the suit and the colors should be conservative—dark blues, blacks and grays. For women, jewelry is understated and shoes are modest—low heels, with toes and backs covered—no peep toes, sandals or slingbacks.

Thankfully fashions do change over time. I mean, I haven't seen a bustle in ages. Fewer and fewer companies require a conservative business attire dress code. But there are some industries that still follow a more formal dress code. They typically include financial institutions and accounting,

---

ETIQUETTE DILEMMA

Q. *My company is having a holiday party. What should I wear?*

A. *Typically, holiday parties are dressy affairs. Ask the party planner what the dress code is. If it's cocktail or semi-formal attire, women can wear a short cocktail dress—one that is dressy yet not too sexy, or a festive suit in an evening fabric. Keep in mind that this is still a business event, so avoid thigh-high slits and down-to-there necklines. Women can wear a higher heel as long as they can walk sensibly. For men, a dark suit, white shirt and dark tie with an understated or holiday pattern is appropriate semi-formal attire. Some parts of the country, such as the West Coast, are more informal, and a tie is not necessary.*

If the dress code is formal or black tie, tuxedos or black suits with white shirts are appropriate for men. Women may wear floor-length or knee-length evening dresses.

---

investment and law firms. Companies that conduct business overseas or with clients in conservative industries also tend to wear business attire. That's because people in most countries outside of the U.S. tend to dress more formally.

Keep These Attire Points in Mind:

- Press your clothes if they are wrinkled.
- Keep your shoes polished. Have a polishing cloth at work if you commute in your work shoes.
- Carry a high-quality purse or briefcase.
- Keep your fingernails short and clean. If you wear nail polish, remove it when it starts to chip or grow out.

ETIQUETTE DILEMMA

Q. *Should my socks match my shoes or my pants? What about my belt?*

A. *A man's socks should match or complement his pants, not his shoes. When you sit down and your pant leg is pulled up, the matching or complementary sock keeps the color line consistent with your pants. Socks should be at least calf-high to avoid showing skin when you sit down. A recent trend is for men to wear more colorful socks. These socks can be a fun accent to your outfit; however, they are best worn either in more casual or creative industries or in social settings.*

Your belt should match your shoes.

A Word about Revealing Clothes

Avoid wearing anything that is body hugging or revealing. This includes shirts or dresses that show cleavage, mini-skirts or dresses shorter than two inches above the knee, or see-through fabrics. Wearing these items sends a sexual message, intentional or not, and can diminish your credibility. Dressing more modestly conveys your professionalism, and puts the focus on your work ethic rather than your body.

No matter what the dress code is, make sure your clothes are clean, wrinkle-free, fit well and are in good shape. If in doubt, don't wear it. Ask your manager or human resources staff for guidelines if there isn't a dress code or it's not very clear. They are there to help.

GROOMING

Good grooming is essential. It goes without saying that you should shower or bathe every day and use deodorant or antiperspirant before getting dressed. Wash your hair often enough that it is never greasy or smelly. For some people that means every day; others can go two to three days between shampoos and still look and smell fresh. Make sure your nails are clean and cut short.

Hair and More

When it comes to men's hair, short, trimmed tresses will never be wrong and will present a well-groomed appearance in any situation. But if you prefer to remain "natural," you have to consider the situation. If you have hair that can appear uncontrolled (thick, bushy or very curly), then a short, trimmed style makes it easier to be presentable all the time. Dreadlocks or hair styled like a rock star might work in some business environments, but your credibility might be challenged in other situations. Whatever your style preference, good grooming is required.

While women have more leeway when it comes to long or short hair, keep hair neatly styled and out of your face. If you haven't gotten a new 'do in a while, it's probably time to update it. The Farrah Fawcett flip or big 1970s-style Afro were great in their time, but sporting those looks today may make you look dated. It's best for women to update their hairstyle every few years.

If your stylist keeps giving you the same cut, despite your request for something different, start looking for a new hairdresser. I know how hard it is to switch stylists, but sometimes change is for the better. For very unmanageable hair, look for someone who specializes in your hair type and who can recommend hair

ETIQUETTE DILEMMA

Q. *I'm meeting with a client who always dresses very casually. How should I dress?*

A. *Don't be tempted to dress as casually as your client; you want to maintain a professional image. Wear a jacket and dress shirt without a tie, if you're a man. A woman can wear a sweater or jacket over a dress shirt or blouse with dress pants. If your client wears jeans and a t-shirt, take your jacket off when you meet. Or, if you work in a more casual industry, you can wear khakis with a polo or knit shirt, but don't wear jeans and a t-shirt. Essentially, you want to dress one step up from your client.*

products that work with your hair. The right cut and product can tame even the wildest locks.

Facial hair for men is typically not appropriate in conservative industries, unless it is part of your religious beliefs. Other industries vary widely on the appropriateness of facial hair, so it is best to consult your company's dress code or ask your manager. If you do have facial hair, make sure it's well groomed.

Women, a few words about makeup: Use cosmetics to enhance your features, rather than create a mask. What does that mean? Essentially, if you are spending more than fifteen minutes putting on your makeup, you're probably wearing too much. Keep your cosmetics understated in the workplace.

Not So Scentsational

When wearing perfume or cologne, make sure the scent doesn't precede you or leave you lingering. If people know you're coming before they see you, please step away from the diffuser. Because so many people are sensitive to scents, it's best to not wear any (including strongly scented deodorant), especially when meeting with clients. Let your winning smile, confident handshake and professional communication leave an impression, not your cologne.

Speaking of scents, be sure your breath is fresh. Some of the worst breath offenders are coffee, peppers, alcohol, tomato juice, citrus juices, garlic, onions and sugary foods.

Brush your teeth and/or use mouthwash to banish bad breath. A mint will help, but it usually won't take away the odor for long. Drinking water throughout the day will keep your mouth rinsed and moist, banishing the bad bacteria.

TYPICAL WORKPLACE ATTIRE NO-NOs

- *Shorts.*

- *Jeans, except for a sanctioned casual day.*

- *Stiletto heels—which are pointed heels that are four inches or higher.*

- *Revealing, tight or low-cut clothes.*

- *Flip-flops or athletic shoes.*

- *Baseball caps.*

- *Clothes that are wrinkled, torn, stained or otherwise meant for weekend chores.*

- *Sweats, sweatshirts, yoga pants or t-shirts with sayings or logos.*

- *Sport socks.*

- *Neon, black or wildly patterned nail polish.*

If you work in the high-tech industry and don't interact with clients, some of those casual items may be perfectly acceptable; ask your manager.

Accessories

If you want to make a good impression, spend a little extra on quality accessories. Attention to detail makes you stand out. For instance, if you hand out your business card regularly, buy a nice business card holder. People will notice it when you pull out your cards. The added benefit of using a holder is that your cards won't get bent or stained in your wallet or purse. Other business-related items you can justify splurging on include purses, belts, wallets and a good pen.

Lastly, if you need to pay attention to time in client meetings, invest in a premium watch. Not only will it communicate your attention to detail, but you'll avoid seeming rude by checking the time on your smartphone during a meeting. Glancing at a high-quality watch is much more acceptable. And yes, a smartwatch is just fine, but do turn off the notifications while you're meeting with others.

ETIQUETTE DILEMMA

Q. *A coworker has terrible body odor. Should I say something?*

A. *That's always a touchy situation. Unless your coworker is a close friend, it's best to inform her manager and let the manager handle it. However, if your coworker is a friend, you could say something in private away from others. Your conversation might go like this: "Mary, you probably aren't aware of this, but you often have body odor. As your friend, I'm telling you so you can do something about it. I know how much you care about your professional image." If Mary seems receptive to talking about it, you could brainstorm ways to curtail the odor: a different deodorant, more frequent showers, using moist towelettes, etc.*

Be kind and helpful. Imagine how hard it would be to hear that you smell. If others are talking about her body-odor problem, keep that your secret. Otherwise, she will feel everyone is gossiping about her, which will make her feel even more uncomfortable.

THE ART OF
EYEBROW SHAPING FOR WOMEN

Eyebrows frame your face. Pluck them too thin and you'll look perpetually surprised or gaunt. Leave them too bushy and they could dominate your face. Brow expert Stacya Silverman says, "Usually, you look best with your natural brows that are neatly groomed. This look is more sophisticated and professional than a severe, defined arch or over-tweezed brow."

For beautiful brows that enhance your eyes, Silverman recommends following these tips:

- *Use a magnifying mirror in a well-lit area. When tweezing, occasionally step back so you can see your brows as a whole. Be conservative with what you remove because brow hair does not always grow back. Better too thick than too thin.*

- *Align the start of your brows with the upper bridge of your nose. Remove only those hairs that are on the bridge of your nose.*

- *Don't pluck from the top of your brows, which can flatten out your natural shape.*

- *To lift your arch, tweeze selected hairs on the underside of the brow about three-quarters of the way from your nose bridge. From the arch, your brows should taper gradually and follow the angle of your eye.*

- *Do not make the ends (toward your temples) into a sharp point, which can shorten your eyebrows and make them look unnatural.*

- *When in doubt, consider seeing a trained brow specialist who can shape and maintain them.*

And if you're concerned that your brows are not identical, Silverman states, "They are sisters, not twins." Let them be unique.

JEWELRY, TATTOOS AND PIERCINGS

The jewelry you wear in the workplace should be modest and not too flashy. If you wear a statement necklace, wear earrings that are small and less showy—and vice-versa. Diamond or pearl studs or small hoops are always a good choice for business. Don't wear rings on more than three fingers.

If you were a wild child and got multiple ear piercings or other body piercings, it's time to tame that wild side. Remove all

---

ETIQUETTE DILEMMA

Q. *What if I spill something on my shirt before an important meeting?*

A. *Darn, that's the worst! Always carry a stain remover for exactly this purpose. It's also a good idea to keep a clean shirt at the office in case of a stain emergency. However, if you have neither, you still have a few options.*

- *Try removing the stain by blotting—not rubbing—it with cold water.*

- *If the stain is still there, apply a small amount of dishwashing detergent. Use a dampened sponge to blot up the soap and stain.*

- *If the stain persists, try to hide it with your jacket, sweater or scarf.*

- *And if that's not possible, simply make a joke about it—"I got into a fight with my coffee this morning and the coffee won." It's better to be upfront about the stain, rather than have your client question your hygiene.*

but up to two earrings per ear and remove any visible body piercings. It may not seem fair, but unfortunately either you won't get hired if you're looking for work, or you won't be taken seriously in the business world.

Before you're tempted to get a tattoo, read the employee handbook or ask your manager if a tattoo is acceptable. Or get one in a place where it's easily hidden.

True confession: In my early years, I got a tattoo of a small iris on my ankle. While I love my tattoo, now that I am an etiquette consultant, I feel somewhat self-conscious about it. You just never know where your career will take you, so err on the conservative side when considering tattoos and piercings.

INTERVIEW ATTIRE

For job interviews, dress a little more formally. Before the interview, try to find out what the dress code is for the company

ETIQUETTE DILEMMA

Q. *Should I hide my tattoos when interviewing?*

A. *While tattoos have gained more mainstream acceptance, many companies will not allow them if the job is more of a professional role or includes working directly with clients. If you suspect your tattoos would hurt your chances of being hired, cover them up. Or you could take a risk by not hiding them during the interview. If the potential employer is okay with tattoos, displaying them won't pose a problem. Other hiring managers either will not hire you or will ask you to cover up while at work.*

where you are interviewing and dress one step up. For example, if it's a more casual company, wear a jacket over a casual shirt with khakis. If the workplace adheres to business casual, wear a suit. A company with a more formal dress code—business attire—would suggest that men should wear their best suit and a high-quality tie. Women need to wear understated jewelry and modest closed-toe dress shoes with their pant or skirt suit, and a silk or synthetic blouse or dress shirt underneath.

Don't wear cologne or perfume to an interview. Some people are sensitive to it.

When getting dressed for your day at the office, ask yourself if your outfit is appropriate for the job you have or aspire to have. Choose those items that make you look and feel like a professional. When in doubt, don't wear it; then consult your manager or HR department for future reference. Your thoughtful approach to your work uniform will make you more respected and promotion-worthy.

ETIQUETTE DILEMMA

Q. *Can I take my jacket off in an interview?*

A. *Feeling a little hot under the collar? I understand. Interviews can make you warm, but to maintain a professional image, keep your jacket on even if your interviewer removes his.*

CHAPTER THREE

HELLO, MY
NAME IS JANE

Meeting and Mingling with Ease

Hope grew up in a small, depressed town in a home with parents who weren't very attentive or supportive. But that didn't stop her. Of the 220 people who started at her high school, only 62 graduated, and of those 62, just 5 went to college. Hope was one of them.

While in college, Hope attended a scholarship-program networking event and found herself standing next to an older businessman. She decided to strike up a conversation. They talked about golf, her past and her future. After an engaging conversation, he revealed who he was—the president of a large bank. He was so impressed by Hope, he told her he wanted her to work for the company. Hope laughed it off, thinking he was joking. He persisted and asked for her business card and gave her one of his. He insisted she send him her resume.

Eventually she sent him her resume and ended up being hired for a management trainee program at the bank. Hope took a risk by talking to the well-dressed professional man at a networking event—and landed a great job.

....

Networking can have huge payoffs, just as it did for Hope. However, most people dislike networking. According to a recent *Seattle Times* survey that asked which was worse—networking or dating—48 percent responded that networking was worse, while only 11 percent responded they disliked dating more. Another 33 percent said they were equally awful.[1]

And yet networking is essential to your success, whether you're looking for a job, clients, investors or a promotion.

Even if you're employed, aren't in a sales position or own a business, it is wise to keep your network active in the event you lose your job or want to work for another company. A strong network is also important so that you can call on your colleagues for support and resources. At the very least, you can expect to attend business and social receptions and parties where you need to mingle. Despite your potential dislike of mingling it is something we all have to do at one time or another.

I know mingling can be hard, but I encourage you to get comfortable with it so that you'll have more success professionally and socially. The following points will help make your networking easier and more beneficial.

NETWORKING ESSENTIALS

Networking is about building relationships, and that takes time. As you cultivate connections, treat networking more as an occasion to get to know people than a sales opportunity. People don't like to feel like a victim of a sales pitch at a reception. Approach mingling as a way to meet and be of service to others. Offer to introduce people you meet to others who might be helpful to them. For instance, perhaps someone you're talking to mentions needing a dog walker and you happen to know someone who offers this service. Introduce the two via email or in person if they are both in the room. Another way to be helpful is to promote the services, workshops, books or awards of your connections to people you meet. Again, you can do this either online or in person. Give before you take. And you know what? You will enjoy mingling more when you're there to help people.

Set Clear Goals

Having goals for the events you attend will help you to be more focused and feel more purposeful. Often when we network we just show up and hope for the best, but when we have a goal it gives us something to focus on besides our nerves. Goals also make our networking more productive.

When you are starting out as a networker, your plan might be as simple as to stay at the event for fifteen minutes, or to talk to two people before leaving. It's okay to start small. As you get more comfortable with networking, your goals may expand. I encourage you to stay away from having the goal of getting X number of clients or getting a job. Remember, networking is about building relationships. If you approach it as a sales opportunity, whether you're selling yourself as a job candidate or you're peddling a product or service, you likely will have little success.

If you are looking for a job, an appropriate goal might be to talk to three representatives from companies you're interested in and to learn more about them and their needs. See the difference? You're not trying to convince the representatives to hire you; you're simply getting to know them. This takes the pressure off, and that will make you more relaxed.

....

MINGLING COURTESY

When you're talking to others and notice another person is trying to join your group, be open and helpful. Smile and move in a way that opens a slot in the group and encourages others to join the conversation.

....

Show Up Early

When you arrive early, as people are just beginning to mingle, you'll find it's not as intimidating as walking into a large crowd that has already formed groups. As one of the first to show up, you can serve as a greeter and make others feel more comfortable as they arrive. I much prefer that over walking into a room full of people engaged in conversation with others.

Put Your "Bold" Hat On

When you get ready for a networking event or party, put your imaginary "bold" hat on before you walk through the doors. It's helpful to remember everyone has a hard time introducing themselves to strangers. But that's not an excuse to hold back and wait for others to reach out to you. You won't meet your goals that way. Whether you hope to meet potential clients, make new friends or just have fun, let your bold hat give you courage and confidence—a winning combination when you're networking.

Three or More or Someone Standing Alone

When walking into a mingling situation, it's a good idea to approach groups of three or more, because they tend to be more open to others joining in and usually aren't having a personal conversation. Or, walk up to someone standing alone because she quite possibly doesn't know anyone. Or she may have left her bold hat at home and will be grateful you took the initiative to introduce yourself. Just smile, say hello and make a comment, give a compliment or ask a question, such as, "Have you attended this event before?" Some of my best connections have been with people who were standing alone or who were wandering through the event unaccompanied.

Be Self-Sufficient

For social business events, don't expect the host or hostess to entertain you—be self-sufficient. The host is usually busy and doesn't have time to focus on one guest for long. Make it your responsibility to converse with the other guests and ensure you have a good time. That said, do ask the host to introduce you to a few people. A good host will do that anyway.

I was invited to a milestone birthday party for a high school classmate's husband. It had been many years since I had seen my classmate and even longer since I'd seen her husband. Both my

ETIQUETTE DILEMMA

Q. *How do I pick which networking events to attend?*

A. *It can be overwhelming trying to decide which group or organizational events to attend. There are thousands of professional establishments that host networking events— chambers of commerce, Rotary clubs, Meet Ups, Business Network International (BNI), women's groups, industry- specific organizations and so on. Do a search for networking groups or professional organizations in your area and attend a few meetings that sound like a good fit. The key is finding an organization that aligns with your interests, your job function or your client base. Often you'll find the organizations that fit the best are the ones where you like the people who attend, and you look forward to showing up regularly. When you enjoy the people in the group you will be more natural, which will lead to better relationships. And the more often you attend, the faster you'll build those relationships, which ultimately helps you with your goals.*

husband and I were invited, but my husband wasn't able to join me, so I was on my own.

I was dreading the party as it drew closer since I knew I wouldn't know many people attending. But I gathered up my courage, put my bold hat on and walked into my classmate's lovely home, fashionably late but still before most of the crowd had arrived.

I saw the birthday boy talking to a couple, so I walked up to this group of three, waited for him to see me, and said hello. He then introduced me to the couple, and we started conversing.

A little later, my classmate saw me and said hello. We talked briefly, but I knew she was busy, so I didn't try to keep her to myself. I made a point of being self-sufficient. Throughout the evening, she did a good job of introducing me to people who happened to be near her when she did pass by me. She was the perfect hostess.

Eventually, more of my classmates arrived. One, who is out-going and friendly, confided in me that she is very uncomfortable mingling. I shared with her my three-or-more rule and that often when I approach a group, I'll say something like, "You look like a fun group." My classmate said she could never do that. Once again, I was reminded that networking success has nothing to do with how gregarious you are. It is much more about your willingness to step out of your comfort zone.

Despite my own nervousness, I introduced myself to several strangers at the party, and I not only survived, I thrived. Something that helps me feel more comfortable is talking to more than one person at a time when possible. I am actually pretty shy, so it takes the pressure off me when there is at least one other person to add to the conversation.

In the end, I was happy I went to the party. I was able to catch up with old classmates and meet some new people. Despite my initial dread of attending, I practiced several tenets of good networking and had a great time.

Additional Ways to Make Mingling Easier:

Name tag on the right. When you put on your name tag, position it a few inches below your right shoulder. When you shake hands with people, they automatically look up your right arm, and your name tag will be easier to see.

Food and drink finesse. Most people go straight to the bar or buffet when they attend a reception. But what happens when you do that? You either get stuck there or you end up drinking too much. Before you know it, you're no longer in mingling shape. Instead, walk into the room and find a group or a person standing alone and introduce yourself. You can get a drink when you're ready to excuse yourself from the conversation.

If you know you're going to be hungry, try to eat something before you attend the event. If you aren't able to do that or are simply too tempted by the hors d'oeuvres,★ take yourself out of circulation to eat. It's difficult to juggle a plate of food in one hand, a drink in the other, and shake hands at the same time. Actually, it's pretty much impossible, so don't try it.

If I'm enjoying a conversation with someone, I like to ask her to join me for a bite to eat at a place where we can set our plates down. That way we're both indulging, and it's not as awkward as eating alone.

★Fancy French word for bite-sized delectables that taste better when they aren't called appetizers.

How to Juggle a Drink and Plate of Food in One Hand

If you're determined to carry both a plate of food and a glass while mingling, try this technique for holding them both in one hand:

- Put the plate between your ring finger and middle finger of your left hand.

- Rest your glass on the edge of the plate, holding it with your thumb and top two fingers.

ETIQUETTE DILEMMA

Q. *What should I do if I start to shake hands with someone but I don't get my hand fully into his hand? It's always embarrassing.*

A. *This happens to everyone. If the person is someone you don't know well, just let it go. If you know the person, you could say something like, "Oops, let's have a do-over. I didn't get my hand in there."*

- Tuck a napkin between your pinky finger and ring finger if you like.
- Eat or drink with your right hand and easily shake hands with others.

CONVERSATION SKILLS

*You can make more friends in two months by becoming
more interested in other people than you can in two years by
trying to get other people interested in you.*

—*Dale Carnegie*

Have you ever wondered what to talk about while networking? If so, you're not alone. A lot of people struggle with small talk. Conversation is less about talking and more about listening, asking good questions and showing a sincere interest in the other person. People who are good listeners are usually seen as great conversationalists. That's because most people enjoy talking about themselves when someone seems truly interested in who they are.

The Four Levels of Conversation

As you are conversing with people, it helps to keep in mind that there are four levels of conversation. These levels are determined by how safe you feel with the other person and your level of trust.

- The first level is **small talk**. This is the stage most people start with when conversing with strangers. Small talk includes topics that anyone can talk about such as the weather, noncontroversial current events, sports, movies and popular culture. Small talk is important for finding common ground and making a connection.

- If you feel comfortable with each other during small talk, you might move to the next level—**facts**. At this stage, you share information about what you do for work, your family and your interests, without sharing your feelings about these subjects.

- The first two conversation stages are important precursors for stage three because you need to establish trust before you can feel comfortable opening up and risk being judged by others.

- The third level is **opinions**. At this level, you share what you think about various topics—the new restaurant, a sports team or the latest popular TV show. This is also the level where you might discuss controversial topics, such as politics and religion. However, I caution you to stay away from these subjects with people you don't know well. Religion and politics are such emotional topics, they really should be discussed only with people you know and trust and who you feel are receptive to hearing different viewpoints. The workplace is typically not a good place to explore controversial topics.

- The fourth level gets into **personal feelings**. You might share your excitement for a new job or your fear about an upcoming presentation. It's unlikely you will go to this level with someone you just met. Some people never feel comfortable sharing this sort of information with anyone but close friends or family members.

- All four levels require good listening skills, but especially at this level. It's very important to listen with empathy and understanding when people are open and vulnerable.

Here's a sample conversation starting with small talk and moving into opinions:

Jane. "Beautiful day, isn't it?"

Tim. "Yes, the sun makes everything seem nicer." Pause. "Have you attended this conference before?"

Jane. "No, this is my first time. The speakers and breakout sessions seem really interesting. I'm looking forward to attending some of them. How about you, have you attended this conference before?"

Tim. "This is my second time. I attended when it was in Orlando two years ago. The organizers do a great job. They bring in quality speakers and make sure there is something for everyone."

Jane. "Oh, that's good to hear. I'm happy to know the hype about the conference is real. My name is Jane Smith, by the way. I work for Exceed Credit Union."

Tim. "Nice to meet you, Jane. I'm Tim Davis with Visa. If you're still deciding on the break-out sessions, don't miss

ETIQUETTE DILEMMA

Q. *If someone is sick and wants to shake my hand, do I need to shake his hand and risk catching what he has?*

A. *You never want to make someone feel bad for wanting to connect with a handshake. If you know you can wash your hands shortly after greeting the germ-bearer, go ahead and shake. If you aren't able to disinfect your hand right away, say something like, "I'm getting over a cold and don't want to give you my germs. Let's pass on the handshake." You could put your right hand over your heart while saying this to both soften and reinforce the request to not touch hands.*

any presentation by Maria Ellington. Her topics are always interesting, and she's a great speaker."

Jane. "Thank you, Tim. I'll be sure to catch her session. Well, it looks like the first session is starting. I don't want to keep you. It's been nice talking with you. Perhaps I'll see you at lunch."

Tim. "Thanks, Jane. Nice talking with you as well. I hope to see you again."

Early on in my business, I was feeling isolated as a solopreneur without coworkers I could socialize with. I attended a networking event where I saw a woman I had met briefly a few months earlier. She asked me how I was doing, and I decided to be candid and said I was feeling lonely not having coworkers around. She said, "I know what you mean, I feel the same way." We then talked about how we were feeling and the challenges of being sole proprietors. I felt close and safe with her, and we made a nice connection.

A few days later, I attended another networking event, and I struck up a conversation with a woman there. We started with small talk—talking about the group—and moved to facts, sharing information about our businesses. Again I moved to conversation level four, as I had done a few days before, sharing personal feelings by stating I was struggling with feeling lonely as a business owner. This woman responded by saying she never feels lonely and that she has many friends.

I realized that she was uncomfortable with my going to conversation level four when we really didn't know each other. She was not ready to discuss personal feelings with me, so she essentially stopped the conversation by saying she never felt lonely. Consequently, I took the conversation back up to small talk and excused myself after a short time.

We did not have the same connection or sense of safety that I enjoyed with the first woman with whom I shared my feelings. And that's okay. It was a good lesson about the risk of going from conversation level one to level four with a stranger in one discussion. Most people aren't comfortable with that. But if they are, connecting at level four can deepen a relationship more quickly.

In fact, when you risk being vulnerable with others, it often helps to make a stronger connection because you have dropped your everything-is-perfect mask. You become more real and relatable, and that allows others to do the same. I encourage you to be yourself when you're networking.

While you don't want to discuss your dysfunctional childhood with a stranger, you might say you're feeling a little nervous because you don't know anyone at the reception, or you could share the anxiety you're feeling about your upcoming work presentation. Most people can relate to those feelings and will feel safe sharing their own fears about similar situations.

Timing is Everything

When networking, plan to spend no more than five to ten minutes talking to each person. Usually you'll run out of topics to discuss after ten minutes. Besides, you want to continue mingling so that you can meet more people. But you can't just walk away from someone. You need to end the conversation in a friendly way. Many people struggle with how to do this.

Ending Conversations

There are two parts to ending a conversation. The first involves the reason for moving on. You might say you want to keep mingling or that you need to freshen your drink. (Be sure your drink isn't full!) Or you could mention that you see someone you need to talk to.

The second part of ending a conversation is what I call the "gracious close." This is when you say something such as, "It was nice talking to you. I hope to see you at another event." Even if the person was boring or you couldn't make a connection, it's important to make him feel good about the conversation. You can state the reason and the gracious close in any order. For example, "I've enjoyed talking to you; I promised myself I'd talk to three people tonight, so I best keep mingling. Enjoy the rest of the event."

Another courteous way to end a conversation is to introduce your conversation partner to someone else. You might say something like, "Joe, have you met Mary Howard? She just returned from Italy and could give you some ideas on where to go when you visit. Mary, Joe Smith and I were just talking about his upcoming trip to Italy." Once they start talking you can make your exit. "It was nice talking to you, Joe. Have a great vacation."

ETIQUETTE DILEMMA

Q. *What if the person I'm talking to discusses something I know nothing about? I don't want to sound uneducated.*

A. *We can't be experts on all topics. Simply admit your ignorance on the subject and ask your conversation partner to tell you more about the matter. Rather than judging you for your lack of knowledge on the topic, she will be flattered you are interested in her expertise. People love talking to an interested listener.*

Don't Scan

Never scan the room while talking to someone. It's disrespectful to the person you're conversing with and will make her feel she is boring or unimportant to you. Give the person you're talking to your full attention until you part ways.

BUSINESS CARD ESSENTIALS

As you're mingling, you'll most likely be handing out your business card. Americans tend to treat business cards pretty casually. We often distribute them willy-nilly without considering if the card is wanted. Instead, it's best to wait to be asked for your card before giving it to someone. Or, if you feel the person you're talking to is interested in your product, service, company (or just staying connected with you), ask if you may give her your card. And if you are interested in staying in touch with someone, be sure to ask that person for his card.

Face It Toward Them

When you hand someone your card, do so with the information facing him so that it's easier to read. And when you accept a business card, slow down a bit and look at it. If possible, comment favorably on the card before putting it away. This is courteous and shows interest in the other person.

Be Careful Where You Put the Cards

Where you put the card you receive also sends a message. It's best to put it in a business card holder, a notebook, a suit jacket pocket or a top shirt pocket. Avoid putting it in your wallet and placing your wallet in your back pocket. This is especially insulting to people from Asian countries and could cost you the business relationship.

Don't Deface Other People's Cards

Never write on a person's business card in his presence unless he suggests it by saying something like, "Let me give you a better phone number to reach me." If the person you're talking to asks you to follow up about a matter, write his name and what you've promised to do on a notepad unless he encourages you to write on his card. Writing on someone's card is similar to defacing that person's property. If you want to remember details about the person, wait until you are out of his sight and then it's fine to write down information on his card that will help you remember him. You might record where you met, what you talked about or any interesting facts about the person. You could also include a description of the person. If you're a forgetful person, take frequent breaks where you can write what you remember about each person on the back of their card without them seeing you. I like to wait until I'm in my car after leaving the event to write my notes.

Protect Your Cards

To present a professional image, be sure to carry your business cards in an attractive business card holder. In addition to making you look sharp, this also protects your cards from being bent or stained. Because your cards are a representation of you, you never want to hand someone a business card that looks as if it has been at the bottom of your purse or is curved from being stuck in your wallet. Make sure your cards are up to date with no information crossed out or written over.

Don't Leave Home Without Them

Lastly, be sure to always carry a supply of your business cards. You never know when you might meet someone who is interested in staying in touch. Even if you're unemployed, I encourage you to print business cards to hand out. Business cards legitimize you and allow people to stay connected. And, you never know when there might be a door prize you want to enter.

MAKING INTRODUCTIONS

When you are mingling, it's important to introduce people to each other. It helps individuals to feel included and makes it easier for them to meet others.

In business, introductions are based on authority, not gender or age. So, when introducing two people, honor the person with the most authority by saying her name first and by introducing the other person to her. Let's say you were introducing the CEO of your company to a new manager. The introduction would go like this: "Mary Smith (CEO), this is Joe Davis (manager)." Or you could say, "Mary, this is Joe Davis, our new IT manager. Joe, this is Mary Smith, our CEO."

There is an exception to the authority rule when you're introducing clients or customers to anyone in your organization. The client or customer is the most important person because she is your bread and butter, so honor the client by saying her name first, even if you're introducing her to the CEO. For example: "Samantha (or "Ms. Jones"), this is Mary Smith (or "Ms. Smith"), our CEO. Mary, this is Samantha Jones, our client from Austin."

If two people have equal authority, it doesn't matter whose name is stated first. Sometimes it's situational. You might be talking to someone and when another person walks up it may feel more natural to first say the name of the person you were talking to. Either way is acceptable.

Always stand when making business introductions, unless everyone, including the introducer, is already seated. Typically everyone stands unless you are elderly or frail. It's a sign of respect and equality.

To make a great introduction, share some information about each person. Maybe where they work, hobbies they enjoy or interests they have. You could also mention how you know each person. This gives the people you're introducing something to talk about. For example: "John Davis, this is Carolyn Smith. Carolyn and I met at the Seattle Marathon several years ago. Carolyn, John is passionate about triathlons but has expressed interest in trying a marathon. I bet you could share some tips with him." Once you've made the introduction and the two are talking, you can excuse yourself and continue mingling.

NETWORKING FOLLOW UP

Meeting people at a networking event is just the beginning of building a relationship—you want to follow up and stay connected with the people you meet. The first thing to do is invite people to connect with you on LinkedIn, which is

ETIQUETTE DILEMMA

Q. *What do I do if I forgot my business cards and someone asks for one?*

A. *You can ask the person requesting your card for one of hers and then follow up with her later with your contact information. Never write your information on someone's card unless she suggests doing so.*

the most appropriate social-media site to use for business connections. When you send the connection invitation, be sure to personalize the message. Avoid using the LinkedIn default message. In order to personalize the message, you'll need to go to the person's profile and click on "Connect." It will then ask you to choose how you know the person, and you'll see a default message below that. Go ahead and replace the default message with your personal message. Remind the person where you met and maybe what you talked about.

Next, you could invite your new contact to have coffee or lunch with you. This is an effective way to get to know someone better and talk in more depth without the pressure of a networking situation.

Try to stay in touch with your new friends. You can email links to articles you think they would be interested in. You can also send handwritten notes with pertinent news clippings or congratulate your contacts on a new job, promotion or award. If you know their birthday date, send birthday cards.

Be sure to send thank-you notes, preferably handwritten, anytime someone does something nice for you—a referral, job lead, favor or gift. A handwritten thank-you note is a very powerful way to stand out and make someone feel special. I realize fewer and fewer people send them in our ever-connected email, social media, texting world, but that's exactly why a handwritten note makes you rise above everyone else. Think about it. When you collect the mail, what's the first item you open besides a check? You open the letter that is hand-addressed and looks like a card as opposed to a bill or direct-mail piece. However, if handwritten notes are just not your style, at least send an email expressing your appreciation for the person's help.

OFFICE PARTIES

Throughout your career, most likely you will attend company parties. The corporate event can be a wonderful time to make and strengthen connections. It can also leave you embarrassed, disgraced and possibly even fired for your lack of good judgment. Avoid these seven pitfalls to stay in your company's good graces:

1. Dressing Inappropriately

Follow the attire description on the invitation. If it's a company picnic, wear more casual, yet modest attire. The company holiday party, on the other hand, is a festive event and one that often calls for dressy clothes, not jeans and a t-shirt. For women, a conservative cocktail dress or festive pantsuit spiced up with a colorful scarf or fun jewelry is appropriate. Be careful not to show too much skin. Remember, this is a business event; don't leave people questioning your judgment. For men, a dark suit is always fitting with or without a tie, depending on the formality of the event.

2. Overindulging

While the drinks may be free, this is no time to let loose. Either pass on the alcohol or limit yourself to no more than two drinks. Uninhibited, you never know what might come out of your mouth, and you don't want to find out the next day through the gossip grapevine or by receiving a pink slip.

A business associate shared a story about one of his clients who put on a big party for employees and company advisors. There was an open bar, and as my associate said, "Big mistake. One employee got abusive and was canned the next day. Another passed out with his head in his plate of food." Yikes, bad news all around! Don't be like those guys.

3. Excessive Eating

The chicken skewers or mini quiche may be the best ever, but avoid eating as if it's your last meal. Unless the event features a full dinner, don't expect to make a meal of the appetizers. It's best to eat something before you arrive. You don't want to look like a glutton, nor have a greasy hand and a mouthful of canapés when Ms. Executive Vice President approaches.

4. Coming Late and Leaving Early

Spending several hours with your coworkers dancing to "She's a Brick House" or doing gunny sack races may not be your idea of a good time, but attending the corporate holiday party or summer picnic is pretty much a requirement. Often your boss and coworkers will notice your absence and might make a mental note that you're not a team player.

Arrive within thirty minutes of the starting time and stay at least one hour. Senior managers will need to be there the majority of the time since the event is essentially hosted by them.

5. Bringing an Uninvited Guest

Be sure to ask if guests are allowed. If they aren't, be polite and honor that request. However, if you are allowed to bring

ETIQUETTE DILEMMA

Q. *What if people in a group I approach don't seem interested in including me?*

A. *Simply make an excuse to no one in particular and leave the group. Don't take it personally. There are plenty of people out there who are welcoming and interested in meeting others.*

a guest, do make an effort to introduce her to your colleagues. Avoid boring your guests by talking business in their presence. Actually, try to stay away from talking business with anyone; remember, this is a social event.

6. Not Mingling

It's tempting to talk to only the people in your workgroup or to those you know best, because it's easier than talking to people you don't know well. But I encourage you to make an effort to mingle and talk to others, including upper managers. This is a great opportunity to increase your visibility and make a good impression on senior-level employees. Ask them about their hobbies and interests or their holiday or summer plans. Stay away from talking shop or carrying on about your kid's Little League average. This is your chance to get to know these busy people—and for them to get to know you. Limit conversations to about five minutes, and be sure to thank the hosts for the event.

ETIQUETTE DILEMMA

Q. *What do I do if I need to introduce someone whose name I have forgotten?*

A. *Don't make a big deal about it. Simply say, "I apologize, I can't recall your name. Will you remind me?" People forget names all the time; it's much better to admit it and move on rather than a) ignoring the person, or b) trying to be clever— "How do you spell your name?" or c) profusely apologizing and making a scene.*

7. Discussing Taboo Topics

There are a few topics to always avoid in a business setting, especially one where alcohol is involved, which will only fan the flames of a heated topic. Stay away from politics, religion, sex, health problems, money or tasteless jokes that are hurtful or mean-spirited. Even if you're sure someone shares your views, you never know who can hear you. Just don't go there. Also avoid gossip or complaining. Keep in mind you're there to have fun.

Networking and mingling will always be something we should do. Practicing some techniques will make it easier and more productive. Keep in mind that most people are uncomfortable mingling, especially with strangers. You will succeed when you put on your bold hat, act with integrity and show your interest in others. Make your fun *your* responsibility, and you'll soon find these events enjoyable.

CHAPTER FOUR

IS THAT YOUR WATER GLASS OR MINE?

Mastering the Business Meal

At a networking luncheon, I noticed the woman to my left pick up the breadbasket and ponder which bread plate belonged to her. After a moment she said to no one in particular, "I think it's this one." She placed her roll on the bread plate to her right. As the bread was passed, others assumed she knew what was proper, so they placed their rolls on the bread plate on their right as well. When the basket reached a young woman she said to the table, "I know which bread plate to use; I learned a trick in a college etiquette class." She then confidently placed the roll on the left bread plate and shared the trick with the table.

A lot of business is conducted over a meal—deals are signed, partnerships are formed and job offers are made. Having good manners and knowing how to conduct yourself, as a host or as a guest, at a business meal will ensure you are more relaxed and polished. This will translate into greater success with the business at hand.

Let's start with a few dining etiquette basics that apply to dining both for business and for social events.

NAPKIN ETIQUETTE

- Put your napkin on your lap as soon as you sit down. If the meal is hosted, wait until the host puts his napkin on his lap. If the napkin is folded in a triangle, unfold it under the table and refold it into a rectangle. That way your lap is better covered in the event of spills, something I experience a little too often.

- Your napkin has three jobs and only three jobs—to wipe your mouth, to wipe your hands and to protect your lap from spills. It should never be used as a food receptacle or handkerchief. More about that later.

- Use your napkin to blot your mouth often, especially before you take a drink from your glass so that you don't leave greasy lip prints or lipstick on your glass.

- When you get up during the meal, put your napkin on the seat of your chair. At the end of the meal or program when you're ready to leave the table, put your napkin on the table, crumple it up a bit to hide any stains and place it to the left of the plate. Never put your napkin on your plate.

- If you are attending a presentation, keep your napkin on your lap during the program, even if you are finished eating. You want to avoid putting a soiled napkin on the table for everyone to look at during the presentation.

NAVIGATING THE PLACE SETTING

Confusion often arises about which items belong to you or your neighbor on a crowded table. Perhaps you've attended a lunch or dinner meeting where someone used your bread plate. Or maybe you weren't sure which coffee cup was yours and used the wrong one, causing everyone else to use the one intended for their neighbor. This happens a lot.

Let me share a handy trick that will keep you from ever wondering which items to use. This is the same tip that the young woman at the networking luncheon shared with the table in the chapter opening story. When you sit down, put your left index finger and thumb together to make a small "b" near your lap so others can't see. With your right hand do the same and make a small "d." Let the left "b" remind you that your **b**read plate is on the left. The "d" on your right hand tells you that your **d**rinking glasses of any type are on the right.

Another way to remember this is the acronym BMW: Your **Bread** plate is on the left, your **Meal** is in the middle and your **Water** (and any other glasses or cups) is on the right.

You may find the plethora of silverware confusing. Here are a few more tips to keep you from faltering.

Use the utensils farthest from your plate first and work your way in toward the plate. This is described as "outside in."

In an informal place setting, the salad fork, which is usually the small fork, is typically farthest from the plate on the left side. The main-course fork, which is usually bigger, is next to the plate. On the right of the plate, you may have a soup spoon farthest from the plate and then the knife next to the plate.

Not to confuse you, but sometimes hotels and restaurants put a teaspoon between the soup spoon and the knife. Depending on the meal, that teaspoon could be for stirring your coffee or iced tea, or it could be for dessert. Traditionally, the dessert fork and spoon are placed above the plate, or they are brought out to you when dessert and coffee are served.

BREAD AND BUTTER

When taking butter for your bread from a butter dish, put it on your bread plate, not directly on your bread. Avoid slicing your roll in half and buttering the whole portion or putting butter on the outside of your roll. Instead, whether it's a roll or a slice, tear off a small piece, butter just that piece, eat it and repeat. And, did you know that your piece of bread can help you push food onto your fork? Yes indeed!

A friend shared with me that she'll never forget the time when she was a teen and was invited to dinner at her boyfriend's house. When she sliced her roll with her knife and buttered the entire half, her boyfriend announced loudly enough that everyone could hear that she was eating her bread wrong. She was mortified. But she told me that she has never buttered her bread that way since. She also broke up with that fellow and later married a great guy who doesn't correct her manners, because that's just wrong.

····································

BUTTER PACKETS

*If butter comes in a butter packet, slide the whole pat
off of the wrapper with your knife and place it on your
bread plate. Fold up the wrapper and put it on the side
of your bread plate.*

····································

SOME TABLE-MANNERS ESSENTIALS

Slow Down

Eat slowly with your mouth closed. And never talk with food
in your mouth. If you're asked a question while chewing,
hold a finger up to indicate you're chewing. If you're being
interviewed over a meal, be sure to take small bites so you can
chew and swallow quickly and answer questions.

Avoid the Boardinghouse Reach

Rather than reaching for items, heed the "rear-end rule." If
you have to lift your rear out of the chair, the item is too far
away. Instead, ask to have it passed. Say, "Will you please pass
the bread?"

Watch Your Posture

Sit up straight in your chair and bring your food up to you,
rather than bending down to the food. I had a boss who would
sit down with a heaping plate of food, lean over the plate and
shovel the food into his mouth as though he hadn't eaten
in days, and say nary a word until he polished off the meal.
Needless to say, this made it very unpleasant to eat with him—
and left a negative impression on his dining mates.

Salt and Pepper

Salt and pepper are always passed together, even if someone asks only for one. Think of them as best friends; they never want to be apart. When passing salt and pepper, avoid putting your hand over the top of the containers, which would leave germs on them. Instead, put a shaker in each hand and pass them to the person sitting next to you, who passes them in a like manner until they reach the person requesting them.

A Few Foods to Avoid

Have you ever labored over lobster or splattered spaghetti? Those are challenging foods to eat. When you are dining for business, avoid ordering these and other difficult items so you can focus on your companion and not the food or your messy fingers. Stay away from these items:

- Large and/or saucy sandwiches, including hamburgers.
- Crab, lobster and shrimp with their shells on.
- Artichokes.

ETIQUETTE DILEMMA

Q. *What do I do if someone takes my bread plate and I have only one on the right of my place setting? Or what if everyone is confused about which bread plate is theirs, and I don't have one at all?*

A. *If your left bread plate was taken, simply place your roll on the edge of your dinner plate. If you'd like butter, you can take a pat from the butter dish and put it next to the roll on the rim of your dinner plate.*

- Whole cherry tomatoes.

- Tacos—hard or soft, they are messy and hard to eat gracefully.

- Sushi—probably best not to take a guest to a sushi restaurant unless you know you are both pros at eating this Asian delicacy.

- Whole fish.

- Finger food—chicken wings, ribs, nachos, and fish and chips.

- Really cheesy items. Dealing with stringy cheese is almost as difficult as spaghetti.

YOU MIGHT BE SURPRISED TO KNOW...

- *Keep your elbows off the table while food is on it. However, you may rest your pointy appendages on the table between courses.*

- *If food falls onto the table, retrieve it with your fingers and put it back on your plate, not directly into your mouth.*

- *Wait to season your food until you've tasted it. However, it is fine to have the server grind fresh pepper on your food before you've taken a bite.*

FINGER FOOD

With a few exceptions, don't eat food with your fingers unless it is indeed finger food—typically food you find at fast-food restaurants or at picnics. I heard about a newly hired saleswoman who came highly recommended. Shortly after joining the company, this young woman took a client out to lunch and ordered baked salmon. When the meal arrived, she ate the fish with her fingers. The client was so dismayed by this woman's lack of table manners, he told her manager, who then fired her.

EATING STYLES

Did you know there are signals you can use to let the wait staff know whether you are still eating or are finished? Perhaps you are taking a break from eating for a moment, but you don't want the waiter to think you're finished. Thankfully, you can communicate your eating status through your utensil placement—but first, a word about the two different eating styles.

American Style

Americans and Canadians use the American style of eating. Assuming you are right handed, you eat foods that require being scooped or stabbed with the fork in your right hand, tines up. Your left hand stays in your lap, unless you are left handed, then your right hand would stay in your lap. When you want to cut something that requires a fork and knife follow these steps:

ETIQUETTE DILEMMA

Q. *What do I do with an inedible piece of food in my mouth?*

A. *Whether you're dealing with gristle, a pit, a piece of bone or some other distasteful item, take it out of your mouth with cupped fingers and place it on your plate, preferably hiding it somewhere. You may have been told to take it out the way it went in, but imagine spitting a piece of fat or gristle back on your fork. Yuck! Using your fingers allows you to hide it rather than spitting the offensive item onto a utensil for everyone to see. Don't spit the item into your napkin, because it would render your napkin unusable.*

1. Transfer the fork to your left hand with the tines facing down.

2. Pick up your knife with your right hand.

3. Cut one piece of the item.

4. Put the knife down at the top of your plate with the blade facing toward you and transfer the fork to your right hand, tines up, to eat what you cut.

If your head is spinning right now, don't worry. If you are American or Canadian, most likely you eat this way without thinking.

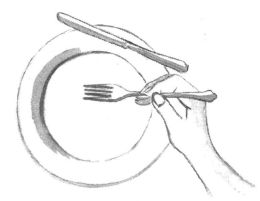

Eating American style

ETIQUETTE DILEMMA

Q. *I found a bug in my borscht. What do I do?*

A. *Eat it; it's extra protein. Just kidding. No matter how disgusted you are by it, do not make a scene. You don't want your dining companions to lose their appetite. Discreetly alert the waiter and ask for a new meal.*

Continental Style

When eating Continental style, or as it's sometimes called, European style, keep the fork in your left hand with the tines down and the knife in your right hand at all times. Your knife is used as a pusher to guide food onto the back of your fork. Bring the morsel up to your mouth with the fork in your left hand with the tines down. Your hands are always visible, unlike American style where your other hand stays in your lap when you're not using your knife.

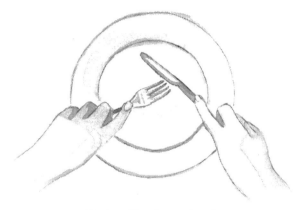

Eating Continental style

Silent Server Codes

Each style has codes that communicate to the waiter if you're resting or if you're finished with your meal.

If you're eating American style and wish to silently inform the waiter that you are still eating, put your knife across the top of the plate, with the blade facing in toward you, and your fork on the side of your plate in the four o'clock position (if your plate were a clock). Make sure the handles of your utensils are not hanging off the plate like oars on a boat.

American style resting position

If you're eating Continental style, place the fork with the tines down at the eight o'clock position on the plate and the knife at four o'clock on the plate, just as you've been holding your utensils.

Continental style resting position

ETIQUETTE DILEMMA

Q. *What do I do with empty sugar or tea wrappers?*

A. *Fold empty or partially empty wrappers and hide them under your coffee cup saucer or bread plate.*

When you want to signal you are finished, whether there is food on the plate or not, put your fork and knife together at the four o'clock position on the plate. If you're eating American style, your fork tines face up. If you're eating Continental style, the fork tines face down.

American style finished position (tines up)

Continental style finished position (tines down)

Now, you might be thinking, does it really matter if my tines are up or down? No. This is not brain surgery. No one's life is on the line. I'm teaching you the proper way to dine, but you get to choose if you want to do it that way or not. The people who will most notice will be those who live or grew up in Europe or were taught formal manners. And in case you are wondering why we do it this way, it is because the position of the fork tines is representative of how you've been holding your fork. It's simply easier to place the fork tines down in Continental style because that's how you hold the fork while eating. The same is true for American style where you eat with the tines up most of the time.

Note: Not all waiters know these codes. Still, I encourage you to practice the codes. You will find wait staff that do understand what you're communicating, especially in more formal restaurants and throughout Europe. If a waiter doesn't seem to know the codes, please don't point out his lack of knowledge. Just let it go.

For the wait staff out there, I'd like to encourage you to refrain from asking, "Are you still working on that?" It sounds a bit like eating the meal is a chore. If you don't see the server codes, ask, "May I take your plate?" or "Are you finished?"

And servers, whether you see the "finished code" or not: If a plate is empty, there is no need to ask the diner if she is finished. You are safe to remove it. However, do not remove plates from the table until everyone is finished. When you remove plates one at a time it makes those still eating feel they need to rush.

CONVERSATION AT THE TABLE

Let's talk about table conversation. You might be surprised to learn that business meals are not about the food. They are about the relationships you build with your dining partners. So keep your conversations pleasant and friendly—not focused on the food. Avoid gossip, complaining and controversial topics: religion, politics, anything that brings up past hurts or is mean-spirited. Other verboten topics include your latest diet, food restrictions and health problems. And make a point to talk to people sitting on either side of you, even if one neighbor is more interesting. If the group is six or less, the entire table might converse about the same topic, or people may break into pairs to talk. Either is fine.

As with any conversation, start with small talk—which hopefully will lead to more substantive talk. Ask open-ended questions that start with *who, what, where, when, why, how* or *tell me*. This will encourage your dining companions to open up more, which will make it easier for you to find something you have in common.

INTERVIEWING OVER A MEAL

Sometimes job interviews are conducted over meals, possibly because the position will entail meeting with clients or VIPs over lunch or dinner. Or, the interviewer wants to ensure your table manners are up to par. Other times, companies schedule interviews over meals because that's the only time they can fit you in, or you're in a full day of interviews and they know you need to eat lunch. No matter the reason, be sure you practice good table manners.

Typically, it's hard to eat and answer questions during an interview. If you can, try to eat something beforehand, so you aren't ravenous during the interview. If you expect to be interviewing for most of the day, bring an energy bar or some nuts for fuel between meetings.

When you walk into the restaurant with the interviewer, wait for her to invite you to sit down. If you're wearing a jacket, leave it on, even if the interviewer takes hers off.

If your host picks up the menu right away, follow suit. Otherwise, chit-chat until she picks up the menu and indicates she's ready to order. The time spent exchanging pleasantries is just as important as the time spent answering interview questions. The host may be seeing how comfortable you are with small talk and building rapport.

When the interviewer does look at the menu, avoid spending a lot of time studying it. Feel free to ask what she recommends. That will give you an idea of both the price range to stay in and what items are favorites at the restaurant, making your decision easier.

Order something that's easy to eat, isn't messy and doesn't require a lot of chewing or manipulating. Some appropriate items include bite-sized pasta such as ravioli, penne or tortellini. Other easy-to-eat foods include a chicken breast, a steak or a fish fillet (but not fish and chips, which is typically finger food), risotto, soup or a simple sandwich that isn't too big or saucy. The item you order should allow you to focus on the interviewer, not on the food.

Once the order has been placed, the interviewer will most likely begin the interview. When your food arrives, wait until she starts eating before you begin. Take small bites that you can chew and swallow easily so that you're able to answer questions more readily. Try to match your interviewer's eating pace. Neither rush nor dawdle while eating.

Let the interviewer dictate the number of courses ordered. Don't order any courses your host doesn't. If she orders an appetizer, salad or dessert, follow suit so that no one is eating alone. Should your interviewer invite you to order first, order just an entrée, not a starter, like soup or salad, with your entrée.

At the end of the interview, thank your host for the meal and her time interviewing you, as you would at the end of any interview. State your interest in the job and the company. Mail a handwritten note within 24 hours of the interview. If the interview is for a high-tech job, it's fine to send your thank-you via email.

HOSTING A BUSINESS MEAL

A business meal is a wonderful way to conduct business because it allows more socializing than a meeting in an office or conference room. As the host, you have a few responsibilities to ensure the meeting goes well and your guest is comfortable.

Select the Restaurant

When organizing a business meal, the host is responsible for suggesting and reserving the restaurant. Give your guest a couple of options that are convenient to him. Ask your companion if he has any food restrictions before you make your restaurant choice. You wouldn't want to take your vegetarian client to a steak restaurant or your gluten-free colleague to an Italian place. Choose restaurants that you know, so you are confident of the food quality, service and noise level. Having dined at a restaurant also helps you to be able to recommend dishes to your guest.

If you are hosting a client out of town and are not familiar with the restaurants in the area, ask your hotel concierge to recommend a few places that meet your criteria. Try to visit the restaurant and familiarize yourself with the seating and menu before your meeting.

Once the date is set, be sure to confirm the meeting with your guest, either the day before or on the morning of the meeting. Simply send an email stating something along these lines: that you're looking forward to lunch at noon at Chandler's on the Pier. Or, call your guest to remind him.

Setting the Stage

Arrive early at the restaurant so you can greet your guest in the reception area and to avoid her having to look for you in the restaurant. If you must wait at the table, you may order a drink, but don't touch anything, so that the table is pristine for your guest. Once your guest arrives, give her the best seat—the one with the view or facing out into the restaurant. Don't face her toward the wall, kitchen or bathroom. If you've invited multiple guests, seat the most prominent guest in the place of honor, which is to the right of the host.

A colleague shared with me that when he was in the corporate world—he's now retired—a junior employee plopped down in the seat with the best view at a business meal with an important client. My colleague was embarrassed. Thankfully, the client seemed understanding, but it could have been a costly mistake.

Avoid the Check Squabble

When the check comes and people argue over who is going to pay, the atmosphere turns awkward. The host, whether female or male, is responsible for paying for the meal. Female clients have shared with me that when they invite a man to lunch, he often feels obligated to pay for the meal, even though he is the guest. To avoid this, make payment arrangements ahead of time.

FUN FACT

Back in medieval days, people ate only with knives. Because of the treachery of the times, one's eating knife was also a weapon. Someone sitting to the right of a surly diner could easily have his throat slit by the evil-doer. As we evolved into eating with a fork and a knife, it became polite to set the knife on the table with the blade facing in toward the plate. Further, when placing your knife at the top of the plate to rest, face the blade towards you. You do this so you don't display the sharp end toward others.

For example, you can give the maître d' your credit card when you arrive and have him give you the receipt to sign as you're leaving. Or, you can instruct the server to put the check next to you, not your guest. The uncomfortable check-grab will be avoided.

Host Responsibilities

As a courteous host, invite your guest to order a drink, an appetizer or salad and dessert in addition to the entrée unless your time is limited. Additionally, give your guest clues about what to order. What you suggest signals the price range you'd like to stay in, as well as which dishes you most recommend. When you're a guest, if the host doesn't make suggestions, feel free to order an entrée in the mid-price range.

To avoid having your guest eat alone or wait while you eat, order the same number of courses as she does. You may have been pining for the tiramisu the restaurant is famous for, but if your guest forgoes dessert, sadly, so must you.

If you are the host, you set the timing of the meal. You are the one in command. Even though the client is always king or queen at a business meal and is afforded deferential treatment, as the host, you are responsible for signaling when to eat. That happens when you pick up your fork or soup spoon or say something like, "Go ahead and eat. My risotto is probably taking extra time, and I don't want your food to get cold."

Be sure you start eating, or signal otherwise, in a timely manner. Avoid keeping your guest or client waiting while her food gets cold. I was invited to lunch by a vendor and when the food arrived she continued to talk without touching her food. I waited for her to start eating since she was the host, but she continued to chat. I waited some more, but finally I started eating and assumed she either thought I was supposed to begin

HONORING YOUR HOST AND FELLOW GUESTS

- Wait for your host or hostess to begin eating or to give a signal to begin before you dive in.

- Avoid collisions by passing food to the right, unless the person requesting the item is closer to your left.

- Match the pace of other guests so that no one is eating alone.

- Find something positive to say about the meal, even if there are things you dislike.

- Never ask for anything you don't see on the table when dining in someone's home. You wouldn't want to embarrass your hosts for not having the item.

- Don't ask if you can eat something on someone else's plate.

- Never correct your friends' manners or grammar, if you want to keep them as friends.

eating first, or was so engrossed in her conversation she had forgotten the food in front of us. It was an awkward moment.

Host responsibilities also include handling problems. If you notice your client isn't eating much, ask her if her meal is all right. If she says it's cold, overcooked or otherwise not right, talk to the waiter to have it remedied.

If there is a problem with the service, never chide or berate the waiter. Instead, you can say to your guest, "The service here is usually wonderful; they must be having an off night." If you must address the problem, do so away from the table and handle it nicely.

I learned from a colleague that one of his friends had lunch with his highly credentialed attorney. The lunch was going well until the attorney berated the waiter. My colleague's friend promptly fired his attorney because he did not want to do business with a bully.

WINE AND TOASTING ETIQUETTE

Ordering alcoholic beverages during a lunch meeting is usually frowned upon. However, it's acceptable to order an adult beverage or two at a dinner meeting. If wine is to be served, you as the host are responsible for placing the order. Don't ask your guest to do so, as she may not be knowledgeable about wine or your price range. That said, if you know your dining companion is a wine aficionado, you may ask her to order the wine for the table. However, keep in mind that when you cede control of the wine ordering, you might end up paying for a very expensive bottle of wine or two.

Ordering Wine Like a Pro

If you are not a wine connoisseur and feel uncomfortable with ordering wine, try this trick: Hold the wine list up to

ETIQUETTE DILEMMA

Q. *If the interviewer orders an alcoholic drink is it okay for me to do the same?*

A. *Unless you're interviewing for a job in the adult-beverage industry it is not prudent to order an alcoholic drink. If your interviewer orders something from the bar, go ahead and request something non-alcoholic so that you have a drink as well.*

the wine steward or waiter and circle the price you'd like to pay while saying, "I'd like something from this region." You've just communicated to the waiter that you'd like a $20 bottle of wine (or whatever price you circled) that fits the meal. A savvy wine steward will know exactly what to bring you and your guests will be impressed with your wine savoir faire.

When you are handed the cork, you do not need to sniff or bite it. Just look at it to make sure it's not falling apart and then leave it alone. When tasting the wine, you will know if it is bad if it smells or tastes vinegary, or musty like wet cardboard or dirty

USING UTENSILS

- Put your teaspoon or soup spoon on the saucer under the cup or bowl when you're not using it; never leave it resting in your teacup or soup bowl.

- When stirring your tea or coffee, avoid making noise when you swirl your spoon.

- Drop a utensil in someone's home? Pick it up, if you can do so without putting your head in your neighbor's plate (or lap), and ask the host for a replacement utensil. At a restaurant, leave it on the floor and request a replacement.

- Don't wave or gesture with your utensils.

- A used utensil never goes back on the table. The table is germy, so is your utensil. You also don't want to stain the tablecloth. Put the utensil on a plate, or if necessary, rest it on a clean utensil on the table.

- Never put a serving utensil in your mouth or use your used silverware as a serving tool.

socks. (Hmm, don't think I've ever tasted dirty socks. Yuck!) Only send wine back if it is spoiled. Returning wine simply because you don't like the taste or want to look important is ostentatious and will not win you any favors with the wine steward—or your guests.

....

DON'T OVERDO IT

Be mindful of how much you drink in a work situation. While a business meeting over dinner may feel more social, it's still business. Stick to no more than two alcoholic drinks so you can remain in possession of your good sense.

....

Toasting

The host of a business or social meal is responsible for making the first toast. Usually a toast is made at the start of the meal. You can also wait to make a toast during dessert.

ETIQUETTE DILEMMA

Q. *I have a colleague who has terrible table manners. He chews with his mouth open, doesn't use his napkin and shovels food into his mouth. Should I say something? I'm afraid his manners are negatively affecting his reputation.*

A. *It may feel like you would be doing your colleague a favor by telling him about his bad manners, but he will probably not receive it well. Best to keep mum and say something only if he asks you for advice. If he is an employee, then yes, say something as you are in a position to mentor and guide him as his boss.*

If there is an honored guest, toast him first. You also may toast the whole group. When delivering a toast, you may stay seated if it's a small group; otherwise, stand up for a larger group. Hold the glass at chest height, look at the person you're toasting and deliver your toast. Keep it short and sweet. Avoid making rude or passive-aggressive comments.

When I attended training at The Etiquette Institute to become an etiquette consultant, our instructor toasted the group over a seven-course meal. She said, "To my future competition, may you have much success." It was short and funny, a perfect toast.

If you would like to make a toast as a guest at a meal, wait until after the host has made her toast to make yours. If the host doesn't make one by the time dessert is served, you may ask her if you may make a toast.

When being toasted, do not pick up or touch your glass until after the toast or it will look like you're toasting yourself. Once you've been saluted, either say, "Thank you," or make a toast in return; *then* drink from your glass.

HOSTING DINNER PARTIES IN YOUR HOME

You may choose to host clients or colleagues in your home. This is a lovely way to get to know your professional contacts. Typically, you would invite only people you know fairly well, and you would not invite your boss to a dinner party unless it was a special client situation.

Ask about Food Restrictions

Ask your guests if they have any dietary limitations when they reply to your invitation or well before the party so you have time to plan. If the restriction is not too difficult to accommodate, try to do so.

One time I forgot to ask about food restrictions and dislikes until the morning of the party. The menu included a mushroom dish as one of the main courses. Much to my dismay, I learned that one of our guests dislikes mushrooms. Eeek! We had to come up with a substitute dish for our fungi-phobic friend only a few hours before the dinner. Lesson learned: Always ask well in advance to avoid those last-minute scrambles.

EATING POLITELY

- Eat quietly and avoid making sounds such as burping, slurping or smacking.

- Avoid dipping your napkin in your water glass or using the glass as a finger bowl.

- Sip your soup without slurping.

- Never blow or put ice in your soup. If it's hot, cool your jets until it cools off a bit.

- Never push your plate away or stack your plates when you're finished eating.

- Avoid "seefood." Don't talk with food in your mouth or chew with your mouth open.

- If you have something stuck in your teeth, try dislodging it by drinking water. If that doesn't work, excuse yourself and remove it in the bathroom. Please, no toothpicks or finger picking in public.

- If your nose starts running, blot it with a tissue or handkerchief, never your napkin. Avoid blowing or honking at the table.

Greeting Your Guests

The person who invited and knows the guests is the person who should greet them at the door. Once you've welcomed your guests and taken their coats, introduce them to your spouse, partner or co-host—who should then offer them a drink, converse with them for a bit and then introduce them to the other guests.

Typically at a dinner party, you'll spend half an hour to an hour mingling over cocktails and hors d'oeuvres in the living room before heading to the dining room for dinner.

Seating

When you are hosting important guests or have a more formal dinner, the seating arrangements are important. The most honored female guest is seated to the right of the host; the most honored male guest is seated to the right of the hostess. If you are a same-sex couple, you would still seat the honored guests to the right of the hosts or hostesses. You can decide what makes the most sense.

ETIQUETTE DILEMMA

Q. *If I am not drinking an alcoholic beverage, can I still join in a toast?*

A. *Yes, it is fine to toast with water or a non-alcoholic drink. However, never toast with an empty glass. Some people believe doing so brings bad luck. It's also difficult to "drink to" someone or something if you don't have anything to sip.*

The host and hostess sit across from each other at the heads of the table. Serve your guest of honor first, and then serve the rest of your guests in a counter-clockwise direction.

Even for less formal dinners, to facilitate mingling and conversation, split up the couples and, if possible, alternate women and men so that everyone is sitting next to someone of the opposite gender. If the party is larger than four people, use place-cards. Try to seat talkative people with quieter people and/or pair up people who might have common interests.

Keeping the Conversation Flowing

As host, you have the responsibility to keep the conversation pleasant and moving along. Ask your guests questions, and share interesting information about your diners with the others so they have something to talk about. Be sure to engage the quieter guests and help them converse with others at the table.

ETIQUETTE DILEMMA

Q. *I have been invited to a dinner party, but I have a food restriction. Do I say something or just hope there's something I can eat?*

A. *Yes, do say something, as long as it's several days before the party, so the host can prepare. If your restriction is easily accommodated, it shouldn't be a problem.*

If your restriction is more challenging, either ask if you may bring an item you can eat or decline the invitation. It is not fair to expect a host to go out of his way to accommodate an unusual dietary constraint.

If someone brings up a controversial topic, simply steer the conversation to a more neutral one. Example: "Joe, there certainly are a variety of opinions on genetically modified foods. I'm excited to share my favorite unmodified coq au vin recipe with you. Shall we make our way to the table?" If that doesn't work, be more direct: "This subject is a bit hot to discuss now. Let's talk about something we can all agree on. This chocolate cake is fantastic, Cheryl. Thank you for bringing it. I would love the recipe."

As you can see, myriad details ensure a successful business meal. Practicing good table manners and etiquette will help seal the deal, and you'll never have to utter Oscar Wilde's woeful words: "The world was my oyster, but I used the wrong fork."

CHAPTER FIVE

CHATTY COWORKERS

Workplace Courtesies

A client called me about an employee with high potential who was a great worker but who didn't present herself well. The company wanted to promote her because of her intelligence and work skills, but they worried about her people skills and her lack of confidence. One of the problems my client mentioned was that the employee wouldn't acknowledge others as she passed them in the hall.

....

The workplace is an interesting microcosm of society. We work with a group of diverse people who come from varied backgrounds, have different values and beliefs, and have dissimilar work habits. Disagreements and friction are bound to arise when we spend about half of our waking hours with our coworkers. To make time in the office productive and positive, it's important that we mind our office manners and treat our coworkers with courtesy and respect.

When I think back to my corporate life, I most enjoyed working with the people who had a positive, can-do attitude. These friendly folks often expressed their appreciation of others, including their managers. In fact, I have some lovely notes from one of these employees, thanking me for mentoring her and giving her interesting opportunities. She didn't have to write the notes, but her good will lingers to this day. Many years later, I still think fondly of her.

MAKING A GOOD IMPRESSION IN THE WORKPLACE

Acknowledge Others

Start your (and their) day off right by acknowledging the people you work with. As you come into the office, say hello to the folks you see as you walk to your desk. It may seem like a small thing, but I guarantee that people notice when you *don't* do this.

In his book *It Worked for Me*, former Secretary of State Colin Powell shared a story about visiting the White House garage. When he showed up, the garage attendants thought he was lost and asked him if he needed help getting back "home." He said he wasn't lost, he just wanted to chat. After a bit, he asked the attendants how they decided which cars got parked deeper inside the garage and which were parked towards the entrance to get out first. "They gave each other knowing looks and little smiles. 'Mr. Secretary,' one of them said, 'it goes like this: When you drive in, if you lower the window, look out, smile, or know our name, you're number one to get out. But if you look straight ahead, don't show you see us or that we are doing something for you, well, you are likely to be one of the last to get out.'"

It doesn't matter if you're interacting with the janitor or the CEO; everyone desires and deserves to be acknowledged.

Be Respectful

Another way to stand out as a great coworker is to be respectful of the people you work with. That means cleaning up after yourself in the kitchen, keeping your voice down when talking in your cubicle or around others who are working, showing up on time to meetings and taking responsibility for things such as the copier jam your document caused.

Use respectful words too. Say "please" and "thank you." It's amazing what a difference those words make. I had to do an email conversion to Google business apps, and the process was quite challenging. I had all sorts of problems with moving my emails to the new platform. Consequently, I was on the phone to Google support quite a bit—often with a support representative named George. George was so polite and kind. He would always use the words "please" and "thank you" and would respond to my expressions of gratitude with "My pleasure." George's graciousness made the frustrating experience much more pleasant. I told George how impressed I was by his courtesy. I was also pleased to give him high marks in the survey Google sent me once my problem was resolved.

CULTIVATING WORK RELATIONSHIPS

- *Greet your colleagues when you see them.*
- *Give credit where credit is due. If you are praised for a project that was part of a group effort, share the recognition with the others.*
- *Show up to work and meetings on time.*
- *Pack a positive attitude when getting ready for work.*

Don't Gossip

Working with people who are different from you can be challenging, but sharing your negative thoughts about others with your colleagues is never productive and can often come back to bite you. Many people feel that if you're gossiping with them you're also gossiping *about* them. If you need to vent, do so at home with your spouse, partner or close, trusted friend.

Avoid Controversial Topics

The workplace is not a place to push your political or religious views. Avoid posting political posters or pictures on your walls or having anything of a political nature in your cubicle or office. Most people have strong feelings about these divisive topics. It can be challenging to discuss them in a civil way, so keep your politics and spiritual beliefs to yourself in the workplace. When you publicly share your partisan views, you can come across as offensive, even harassing, and that can have negative ramifications for your career.

You might assume others share your political opinions, but you might also discover the hard way that they don't. Many years ago in one of my corporate jobs (before I was an etiquette consultant and knew better), I was conversing with a coworker whom I was still getting to know. She brought up another coworker, and I said, "I think she's a ____ (insert political party here)." My new friend said to me, "What's wrong with that?" Thinking she didn't understand what I said, I replied, "Well, you know, a ____ (insert same political party here)." She then looked at me and said, "Arden, I'm a ____ (same political party)." Oh dear, can you say "foot in mouth?" Because my coworker and I had so much in common, I assumed we also shared political beliefs. Thankfully, we still became good friends despite my major faux pas. But I learned from that never to assume anything—and never to discuss politics with people you don't know well, especially coworkers.

Be Mindful of Your Surroundings

A complaint I hear often from my clients involves people talking about sensitive work topics in inappropriate places— such as the bathroom, the elevator, the lunchroom or a cubicle. When having this kind of conversation, think about the people around you. Find a meeting room or private spot where you won't bother others, and where people won't overhear possibly sensitive or confidential information.

One-on-one meetings between manager and employee should always take place in a private place. Otherwise, if you usually meet in a more open space and then move to a private room for performance discussions or disciplinary conversations, the employee (and everyone in the office) will anticipate a negative conversation and be more stressed about it.

ETIQUETTE DILEMMA

Q. *A woman I work with wears a lot of perfume. While I'm not allergic to scents, it's so overpowering that I find it uncomfortable spending time with her. What should I do?*
A. *If you are comfortable talking to her, say something like, "Mary, your fragrance is lovely, but a little strong and heady for me. It makes it hard to concentrate. Could you wear less or perhaps a lighter fragrance in our close quarters?"*

If you are not comfortable saying something to her, talk to her manager, because the scent is probably something others are having a hard time tolerating as well. Let her manager address the issue.

VISITING CLIENTS

Lucky you, you got an appointment with your prospective or current client. Be sure you're on your best behavior and make a good impression on your VIP.

Timing Is Everything

Show up on time to the meeting. It may sound obvious, but if you are late, it signals to your client that you don't value her time—and that starts the meeting off on the wrong foot. Showing up five minutes before your meeting time is best. If you're much earlier than that, wait in your car or the building lobby until you can arrive five minutes before the appointment.

I had a client tell me that my showing up ten minutes early was annoying because she felt she shouldn't leave me waiting, even though I was the early bird. I had always assumed that those I was visiting would greet me when they were ready.

You're Being Observed

Think about the impression you're making on the people you encounter, or who might see you while you make your way to your appointment. A colleague of mine who worked for a major bank had an office window overlooking the company parking lot. One day he noticed a salesman enter the lot, ignore the visitor parking spots and pull into an employee parking space closer to the building. As he got out of his car, he flicked his cigarette onto the pavement. My colleague was so disgusted by this man's apparent disregard for others that he called the coworker who was meeting with the salesman and told him not to buy anything from him.

Always assume you are being observed. Be professional and respectful at all times. Keep in mind you are representing your company.

Greet the Receptionist

When you announce yourself to the receptionist, hand her one of your business cards and state your name, company name and who you are meeting with. Just as you would in an interview, be friendly and respectful to the receptionist. You can be sure she will share her thoughts about you.

Client Meeting Do's and Don'ts

Once your client greets you, shake her hand and let her show you to the meeting room or her office. Wait to sit until you're invited to take a seat. If she doesn't offer to take your coat, ask where you can hang it. You can take your overcoat off, but don't remove your jacket, even if your client is dressed more casually. Maintain a professional image. However, if your client is dressed very informally in jeans and a casual shirt, it is fine to remove your jacket so as not to look too formal.

Feel free to look around your client's office as long as you're paying attention to her. You can learn a lot about a person from the items in her office, and often this can help you build rapport with your client. But don't comment on anything that could be

---

ETIQUETTE DILEMMA

Q. *My boss keeps trying to discuss politics with me. It makes me very uncomfortable, and I don't know what to do.*

A. *Telling your boss how you feel about her actions can be hard to do, but you need to let her know she is making you uncomfortable. Simply say something like, "I appreciate your passion about politics. It's not something I'm comfortable discussing, so would you mind if we avoid that topic?"*

controversial, such as a political poster or photo of your client with an elected official. While it may seem safe, especially if you happen to agree with whatever is on display, the conversation could move toward areas where you don't agree. That can be awkward at best, business-damaging at worst. Better to just keep mum.

It would be fine to comment on a diploma or award of some sort. You can ask about your client's degree or the school she attended. This is especially useful conversation fodder if you happened to go to the same school. Perhaps you notice a book in your client's bookshelf that you read and enjoyed. You could ask if she enjoyed reading it.

When commenting on photos, rather than asking, "Is that your husband (wife, etc.)?" ask, "Is that your family?" This is a safer approach. I heard of a vendor who, when seeing a photo on his prospective client's desk, asked, "Is that your wife?" Turns out it was the prospect's daughter, and the vendor lost the deal.

Stick within your allotted meeting time. If you aren't finished discussing what you came to talk about, ask if the client would like to continue the meeting or finish the discussion another time. Be respectful of her time.

ETIQUETTE DILEMMA

Q. *My coworker talks really loudly in his cubicle. Should I say something?*

A. *Yes, do bring up the subject. Ask nicely if he could keep his voice down, as it makes it hard for you to concentrate or talk on the phone.*

WORKPLACE DO's AND DON'Ts

Keep your coworkers happy by following these sometimes common-sense but often forgotten tips:

- *Always knock before you enter someone's office or cubicle— say "knock, knock" or "excuse me" if there is no door.*

- *Be respectful of people's time. When visiting someone to chat about non-work-related topics, ask first if they have the time. Don't linger too long.*

- *Make sure you're not interrupting someone who is on deadline or focused on a project before launching into a conversation. Start by saying, "Do you have a moment to discuss the xyz project?"*

- *Avoid eating stinky or strong-smelling food in your cubicle. Last night's leftover lamb curry may smell wonderful to you, but most likely will be offensive to others.*

- *Should your document cause a paper jam in the copy machine, or the machine stops working when you're using it, take responsibility for fixing it. Clear the jam, or ask the facilities or IT staff to look at the apparatus if you can't fix it.*

Major Don'ts

- *Don't take office supplies for your personal use.*

- *Don't eat other people's food. The communal kitchen is not your personal smorgasbord.*

- *Don't do personal business during work hours.*

- *Don't look at or post on your personal social media sites while on the clock.*

RECEIVING VISITORS

Treat people visiting your office as you would someone coming to your house. Be a gracious host. Greet your visitor and bring him to your office. Never have your assistant do this, as it looks as if it's beneath you. As you go through doors, lead the way but hold the door open for him. Take his coat and offer him a beverage. Invite him to sit down.

If someone visits your office, come out from behind your desk to shake her hand. Never stay seated behind your desk. And if you are remaining in your office for the meeting, place your chair at the end of your desk rather than sitting across from your visitor.

When offering a tour of your building, stop and introduce your guest to any coworkers who might interact with your visitor.

In meetings, introduce your visitor to everyone in the room. Always state the name of your guest first unless she is a vendor and you're introducing her to someone with more authority. Then you would state your coworker's name first. Example: "Senior manager first name last name, this is guest first name last name."

CLIENT GIFTS

Giving gifts to clients is a nice way to thank them for their business. Make sure your gifts are appropriate and welcome. Many companies do not allow gifts from vendors or items over a certain dollar amount for fear it will look like a bribe or will oblige the company to do business with you. Find out in advance if the company does accept vendor gifts and if you need to be mindful of any restrictions on the value or kind of gift.

A safe client gift is something that can be shared with a team, such as a basket of fruit or box of chocolates. Making a donation to a charity in the company's name is a lovely gesture as long as it's not a political or religious organization.

Avoid sending a gift that has your company logo on it, unless the logo is small and unobtrusive. The gift should be a thank-you, not an advertisement for your business.

GIFT GIVING IN THE WORKPLACE

Exchanging gifts in the workplace can be a nice way to show appreciation to your coworkers. But your gifts should not make someone feel uncomfortable or obligated to give a gift in exchange.

Avoid giving a gift to your boss, unless the present is from a group. Giving your boss a gift that comes just from you can look like kissing up and can make a manager feel he needs to give a gift to you and every employee.

As a manager, you can give employees small gifts, but this is not necessary. A holiday bonus would be an appropriate and much-appreciated gift for all employees if it's within the company budget. Or, take your team out to lunch, and let them know how much you appreciate them.

Gift-giving between employees is fine, but should be done quietly as people who don't receive a present may feel uncomfortable. The better way to approach office gift-giving between peers is to conduct a secret pal exchange where each employee draws a name and anonymously gives a small gift or series of small gifts to the person whose name is drawn.

EXPRESS YOUR GRATITUDE

There are so many ways to make a positive impression on your coworkers, clients and employees. One of the biggest ways is to express your appreciation. Say "thank you" to the person who makes the coffee in the morning. Express your appreciation to your employees for their contributions—his hard work on a project, her teamwork, his positive attitude or her willingness to always pitch in and help. Being thanked is always appreciated.

When acknowledging someone, be specific with your praise. Rather than saying, "Thanks for the good job," share details about what it was the employee did well. For example, if you are praising someone for his work on a project, you could say something like, "Thank you for your can-do attitude on the website redesign project. Despite hitting many roadblocks, you continued to stay positive and persevere. It made the new website a great success." Clear, detailed recognition is always more impactful.

Thank-You Notes

Handwritten thank-you notes are always a nice way to acknowledge someone. It may seem like a dying art, but when you send a note you've personally scribed, people really notice. Your card won't be immediately deleted like an email. I still treasure cards I've gotten from clients and former managers. They really are meaningful.

Consider also thanking your clients and prospective clients. Send a note after a sales call and when they contract with you. Should the client not hire you, send a note of thanks for considering your company. In your card, compliment the competing business they chose instead, and ask your prospect to keep you in mind should they need your services in the future.

I once was contacted by a prospective client who ended up not hiring me, but I stayed in touch. I sent her a few handwritten notes, sometimes with pertinent articles included, and I also touched base by phone. During one phone conversation she mentioned posting one of my notes on her wall and looking at it regularly. This client did eventually hire me, and it was a wonderful partnership.

More reasons to write a thank-you note:

- After a job interview.
- When you hear you didn't get the job you interviewed for.
- When you receive a gift.
- When you're treated to lunch.
- When someone does a favor for you such as making an introduction to a prospective client or hiring manager.
- After dinner at someone's home.
- After an invitation to a sporting event.

Follow these steps to write memorable thank-you notes:

1. Write the message as soon as it occurs to you so that your feelings are fresh. If you wait, you won't feel as inspired and the words won't come to you as easily.

2. Avoid starting the note with "Thank you for…" It's a predictable way of writing a thank-you note. Instead, begin by saying something about the person you're writing to. Make the note about them. Consider these questions: What makes him or her special? What was it about the gift, favor or referral that really moved you? Is the person or gift/favor/referral really thoughtful, creative, tasteful, interesting, talented, etc.? (I learned this approach from Shawna Schuh, the president of People Skills for Sales Results, an executive coaching company that helps professionals excel with people skills.)

3. Sign the note appropriately. With someone you know in a professional capacity, any of the following closings are suitable: Best regards, Sincerely or My Best. For friends or people you know socially or who are close to you, you can sign: Warmly, Love or Your friend.

4. Handwrite the address and stamp it yourself. Don't use a postage-meter stamp.

5. Send the note within three days of the meeting, gift, favor, etc. Don't let it languish on your desk only to be forgotten.

Example of a thank-you note I've written can be seen below.

One of the keys to writing notes is having stationery supplies on hand. I found when I didn't have the materials I'd never get around to writing my notes. I like to order a large quantity of correspondence cards printed with my name at the top from an online stationery store. Sometimes called flat cards, correspondence cards are single cards (without a fold), and are the most versatile. They can be used for thank-you notes, congratulations, thinking-of-you notes, invitations, etc. Note

Arden Clise
Clise Etiquette

Dear Marie,

You are so kind. Your email introduction to your booking agent was perfect and so appreciated! Jane and I spoke and she wants to sign me as a speaker. I'm very excited! Thank you for your help.

Best regards,

Arden

cards—cards that open—are traditionally meant just for thank-you notes. If you do purchase note cards to be used for thank-you notes, don't buy those that say "Thank you" on the outside. Let your words be the thank-you—another tip from Shawna Schuh.

REMEMBERING NAMES

Remember that a person's name is to that person the sweetest and most important sound in any language.

—Dale Carnegie

One of the most impactful ways to be memorable to others is to remember their names. We all love to hear our name. It makes us feel special and important to others.

I used to be bad at remembering names and told myself and others this was the case. Consequently, I wouldn't work at it. I was giving myself permission to not remember names. One day, my neighbor once again greeted me warmly—"Hi Arden, how are you?" and once again I couldn't remember her name.

ETIQUETTE DILEMMA

Q. *I have terrible handwriting. Should I still send handwritten notes, or would it be better to type the message on note paper?*

A. *You have a few options. You could order personalized note paper and type your message on it using a script font that looks like handwriting. You could print rather than use cursive to write your note. Or you could take a calligraphy or cursive class to improve your handwriting.*

I just waved lamely and said "Hi, nice morning isn't it?" It was embarrassing. That was the day I told myself I needed to do something about my recall problem.

Come Up with an Adjective for the Person

Once I heard this neighbor's name again, I decided to come up with an adjective that described her and started with the same letter as her name. In this case it was easy. Her name was Amy, and because she was always friendly, I thought of the adjective amiable—Amiable Amy. I never forgot her name again.

I've since used that technique several times. The outgoing woman at the pool is Gregarious Gertrude. The well-dressed man at my favorite jewelry store is Dapper Dan.

Repeat, Repeat, Repeat

Other methods work as well. Start by repeating the person's name in your head and in conversation three times when you meet. Just about every time I neglect to do this, I forget the person's name. I like to repeat it right away in my head, and then during our conversation I'll try to say it three times—once when I first meet the person, as in "Nice to meet you, Mary," and then sometime during the interaction and again at the end when I say goodbye, "It was really nice talking to you, Mary."

Movie Star Association

Another tactic that works is associating the person with someone famous or well known, or a character in a book or movie. For instance, the woman with the big orange hair named Margie might remind you of Marge from *The Simpsons*. Or, that handsome man named Justin could make you think of Justin Timberlake. When I met a very tall, former NBA player named James, I thought of the book *James and the Giant Peach*.

Visualize the Name

Lastly, you might employ the mental picture method. Suppose you meet a woman named Beth Sparks. You could visualize sparks coming out of Beth's fingers.

What really helps in remembering names is having the desire to do so. If you don't really care about recalling names you won't put the effort into doing so. Trust me, I know.

LET OTHERS SAVE FACE

When I think of the most gracious people, they are folks who let others save face. They don't point out colleagues' mistakes, and they give people the benefit of the doubt. Here's

ETIQUETTE DILEMMA

Q. *I'd like to mail a card to a colleague, but I can't find her address. What should I do?*

A. *I use several tricks to help me track down an address. I start by going to the person's or company website, if one exists, and seeing if the address is listed there. My next step is to go to www.officialwhitepages.com and do a search by the person's name. You need to have an idea of what city she lives in. Or, you can search by the person's phone number, assuming it's listed. If that doesn't work, ask a friend or colleague of the person for the address. The last resort is to call or email your colleague and ask directly for her address. You don't need to state why you're asking for it; you can be vague by saying something such as, "I'd like to send you something."*

a hypothetical example: Perhaps you have an employee who answers a question incorrectly in a meeting. Rather than point out his mistake, wait until you're meeting privately and nicely explain to him the correct answer. He will be thankful you didn't make him look foolish in front of others and will think more highly of you for your graciousness.

You can't choose your coworkers, but you can choose your attitude and how you treat others. When you are thoughtful and kind to the people you work with, your working relations will be easier and more productive.

CHAPTER SIX

WHO CALLED THIS MEETING?

Meeting Manners

A friend of mine worked with an agency her company had hired for a fairly big consulting job. The agency gave a presentation to the executives, which my friend and her colleagues found quite impressive. Afterward, the agency team sat down at the table to answer questions. But during the discussion, all three of the visitors looked at and even typed on their smartphones. My friend got the feeling that using their phones in meetings was probably typical in the agency's corporate culture. The visitors had no problem keeping up with conversation while casually tending to their devices. However, the executive team was not impressed. It was really off-putting to some of the people at the table and played a part in the decision not to use that agency for any further work.

Meetings are important to share information, brainstorm and discuss projects. Too often, though, meetings are poorly run, they take up too much time, the wrong people attend or there's not a positive outcome. With only so many hours in a day, time in meetings needs to be useful and productive so that employees can focus on the business tasks that matter most. To make meetings more effective, participants and meeting chairs must follow good meeting protocol.

MEETING CHAIR RESPONSIBILITIES

Typically, the person who calls the meeting is the facilitator or meeting chair. The chair creates and monitors the agenda and facilitates the discussions. Following these ten steps will make your meetings more productive:

1. Have a Goal for the Meeting

Before you schedule the meeting, determine what your goal or reason is for the gathering. Think through what you want to accomplish or what outcome you want as a result of the meeting. If you can't identify one, don't meet.

Meetings have three purposes:

1. To share information—to convey a change in the organization, policy, people, products, etc.

2. To get information—such as project or department updates.

3. To solve problems—this could include brainstorming, discussion or feedback.

In all instances, be sure meeting participants are clear on the goals and expectations for their involvement in the meeting. If, for example, you call a meeting to discuss the budget overrun, and you state in advance that you expect the participants to help brainstorm ideas on how to address the issue, the meeting will be much more productive. The participants will have time to pull budget information, or at least think through how money is spent in their departments and throughout the company.

2. Schedule the Meeting Thoughtfully

Set meetings up at least one week in advance so that the participants have availability on their calendars and time to prepare. Less involved meetings can be scheduled within two to three days. Avoid scheduling the meeting on a Monday morning or Friday afternoon. Employees are usually organizing the week's tasks on Monday and most people are ready for the weekend by Friday afternoon.

Don't arrange a meeting that is convenient only for you. Make sure the gathering is at a convenient time and place for those attending.

I heard of a manager who would schedule meetings with his team on late Friday afternoons and they would meet on the ferry boat headed to the island where he lived. None of his team lived on the island, so after their manager got off the ferry, they would have to return to the office, wasting their time on a Friday evening. Needless to say, his selfishness was not appreciated by his employees.

3. Choose with Care Who Is Invited to the Meeting

More people do not necessarily make a more productive meeting. Invite only those folks who are crucial to the discussion or goal. If you're discussing topics that require staff with a certain level of authority or expertise, make it clear you need that person in the room, not a substitute.

ETIQUETTE DILEMMA

Q. *What do I do when I forget the name of someone I know really well?*

A. *Believe it or not, this happens to a lot of people. Just make a joke by saying something like, "Mary, this is my best friend, who I know so well I've forgotten what I call her!" And then laugh and move on. It happens.*

4. Have an Agenda

An agenda helps the chair and the participants know the following:

1. What is being discussed.

2. Who is speaking or should be expected to participate.

3. How much time is allotted for each agenda item and the meeting as a whole.

When you have an agenda, people stay more focused and on track. Send an agenda out a couple of days before the meeting with any necessary documents, so the participants have time to review the materials and prepare for the meeting. Below is a sample agenda from a mastermind group I formed.

Mastermind Meeting Agenda
March 13, 8 to 10 AM
World Trade Center,
2200 Alaskan Way, Seattle

1. Welcome—*Arden*
2. Introduction/Question of the day—*Elizabeth, 30 minutes*
3. Business presentation—*Sheila, 10 minutes*
4. Feedback and discussion of presentation—*10 to 15 minutes*
5. Business presentation—*Kim, 10 minutes*
6. Feedback and discussion of presentation—*10 to 15 minutes*
7. Group discussion: *How are people utilizing LinkedIn to build their business?—up to 30 minutes*
8. Next meeting, **Wednesday, April 10, 8 to 10 AM**
   - Question of the day
   - Presentation or topic idea
   - Coffee sponsor

This particular meeting took place in person, but had it been a conference call, I would have included the teleconference number and participant code on the agenda.

5. Appoint a Note Taker

Notes from the meeting capture the pertinent discussions, outcomes or takeaways from the meeting, so that those who couldn't make the meeting can see what was discussed. Notes also remind the participants of anything they committed to doing or action steps they need to take.

The meeting chair should not be the note taker. The chair cannot fully manage the meeting and take notes at the same time. Appoint someone to take minutes, type them up and send them out to those who were invited to the meeting.

6. Start the Meeting On Time
Even If People Are Late

Send the message that you value people's time and won't wait for latecomers. Eventually, latecomers will change their habits.

7. Make Introductions

Introduce any newcomers to the group. In larger meetings, have the participants go around and introduce themselves, what department they work in and, if needed, their titles.

8. Keep the Meeting on Track

The meeting chair is responsible for keeping the meeting moving forward and ensuring the participants stay focused on the agenda. Not always an easy task, but an important one if you want the meeting to be successful.

When people continually take the meeting off course, the meeting is not as productive. To handle talkative Terry, acknowledge something she has said, and then redirect the conversation to the topic at hand. For example, "Terry, I agree, we should have more work parties; it's always great to have some down-time at work. I'd like to ask Jane her thoughts on the budget. Jane, do you have some ideas on ways we can decrease spending in the IT department?"

When I was board chair for the non profit organization PAWS, the executive director and I attended a seminar on running effective meetings. We learned Robert's Rules of Order, a program created by General Henry M. Robert for meeting management. It follows British parliamentary procedure. The first *Robert's Rules of Order* was published in 1876 and continues to be revised as times change. It's a very handy book to help guide you and your participants in meeting protocol. It can be a bit too formal or procedural for more casual or small meetings, but if your meetings are large or could benefit from more structure, following Robert's Rules of Order can help.

9. Involve the Quieter Members of the Meeting

In any meeting, there will be attendees who are more vocal and those who are more reserved. The chair should make sure to ask the quieter participants for their opinions so that everyone in the meeting has an opportunity to share. Doing so allows those who have a harder time speaking up to share their thoughts.

Beth Buelow, business coach, author and founder of the company The Introvert Entrepreneur, shares her expertise on involving introverts in a meeting.

"It's important to recognize that introverts gather their thoughts silently before they speak, whereas extroverts speak to think. That leads to introverts typically being less vocal in meetings. They're engaged, just in a different, less obvious way," says Buelow. "If someone isn't speaking up and you want to hear from him or her, you might say, 'Tom, before we move on, would you like to add anything?' or, 'Carrie, I'd love to know what you think about this.' Invite their participation, rather than force it."

Buelow shared these additional tips for involving introverts in meetings:

- Avoid putting a quiet person on the spot by saying something like "Jeff, you're awfully quiet over there!" And don't force someone to talk who isn't ready or who has nothing to say at the moment. Be invitational, not shaming.

- Make it clear in the meeting if the occasion is a "speak now or forever hold your peace" moment. That way, people know whether they need to speak up at that time or will still have an opportunity to share later.

- As the meeting leader, you have the responsibility to make the discussion easy and safe for everyone in the meeting. Read the energy of the room, rein in the conversation dominators, and create space for everyone who wants to speak.

- Watch the body language of the less talkative members. This can provide strong clues that indicate they want to speak up but can't break in. For instance, someone who was leaning back in her chair leans forward and makes eye contact with you. Or, she raises her eyebrows and takes a breath.

- Incorporate multiple ways to participate in the meeting. Discuss things as a group, have people brainstorm in pairs or trios, and/or give everyone a few minutes to write down their thoughts before sharing. This honors different processing and communication styles and can result in a more productive discussion.

10. End On Time

Even if you have not finished discussing what was on the agenda, stop at the designated time. Be considerate of people's schedules. If you are close to a resolution, ask the participants if they have five or ten minutes more to finish. If the majority of the group does have the extra time, let those who can't stay leave, and let them know you will send updates on anything they need to be aware of. Before you end the meeting, go over any takeaways the participants are responsible for or that need their attention.

MEETING PARTICIPANT TIPS

As a meeting participant, pay attention to the following points to ensure you are presenting yourself professionally and contributing to an effective meeting.

ETIQUETTE DILEMMA

Q. *How do I politely disagree with someone in a meeting?*

A. *The purpose of meetings is to encourage discussion and feedback. However, there is a fine line between being disagreeable and disagreeing. Be very careful or avoid altogether disagreeing with your manager or a senior staffer. Find something to agree about and then offer another approach. Use the "Yes, and" technique, which is used in improv theater. You might say something like, "Yes, I agree the marketing campaign is not as effective as we hoped, and I suggest we try this …" This approach is also useful for brainstorming meetings. Essentially you add something positive to what is being said rather than dismissing someone's ideas or thoughts.*

Get Approval for Substitutes

If you are invited to a meeting and can't attend, check first to make sure sending an employee or coworker would be appropriate. Sometimes it's important only the person invited attends the meeting, other times a representative from your team or department is fine to attend in your stead.

Be Prepared

We are all busy, and too often wait until the last minute to read meeting agendas and notes. Instead, schedule time in your day to prepare for the meeting beforehand so you can be an informed, contributing participant. Be sure to print out the agenda and any documents attached to the meeting email announcement, and bring them to the meeting.

Show Up On Time

Most people are frustrated when they arrive on time to a meeting only to have it delayed by latecomers. Being late is disrespectful to your colleagues. Plan to finish what you're working on at least fifteen minutes before the meeting, so that you have time to gather any materials you need and arrive on time.

WHEN TO HIRE A PROFESSIONAL FACILITATOR

Consider hiring a professional facilitator if you need to discuss something contentious or important or that is not getting resolved. A trained facilitator will objectively help the group navigate the topic and stay on track.

Don't Sit in the Power Spots

Usually the seats next to the chairperson are reserved for the higher-ranking staff members or those who have a major involvement in the meeting. If you are an outsider to the meeting, ask where you should sit.

However, if you want to be sure you're noticed by the chairperson, the best seats are the two in the middle of the table across from each other (seats 3 and 7 in the diagram below) and the one at the end across from the facilitator (seat 5 in the diagram below). Those seats allow you to establish eye contact with the leader and make it easier to participate in the meeting.

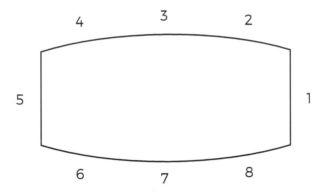

Keep Unnecessary Items off the Table

Have only your note-taking items and the agenda on the table. Stow your briefcase, purse, business card holder, phone and laptop—unless your company culture allows you to take notes on a laptop or tablet.

Don't Undress

Men, keep your tie and jacket on in the meeting unless senior members remove theirs. Then you may follow their lead. Hang your jacket on the outside of the chair.

Women, avoid showing bare arms in client meetings or in a more conservative industry. If you are wearing a sleeveless shirt or dress, keep your jacket or sweater on. You will look more professional and credible.

Never Ask for Food or Drink You Don't See

Always wait to be offered a beverage or food item before requesting anything. Also, don't bring food to a meeting unless it's clear that is acceptable. If the meeting does include food or beverages, remove your plate and glass from the table as soon as you're finished so the surface stays clean and uncluttered.

Watch Your Body Language

Be sure to sit up straight and avoid slouching in your chair. Your good posture will help you stay and look attentive. Keep your feet on the floor and your elbows off the table. Never hold your head up with your hands, making it appear as if you're bored or uninterested. Avoid crossing your arms, which will make you appear angry or defensive.

ETIQUETTE DILEMMA

Q. *When should I hand out my business card in a meeting?*

A. *Typically, business cards are distributed at the beginning of the meeting. Carefully hand out your cards rather than throwing them across the table like you're dealing a deck of cards. Make sure the recipient sees you hand her your card. When you receive a card, take time to look at it, which will help you to remember the person's name and title. Place the cards you receive in front of you to reflect how people are seated so you can glance down and remember who is who.*

Don't Fidget

Avoid drumming your fingers, tapping your feet, and playing with pens, paper clips and the like.

Stay Focused

Strive to keep your mind from wandering off and missing what is being said. There is nothing more embarrassing than being asked a question when you are not paying attention, and having to ask that the question be repeated. If you're having a hard time paying attention, take notes or participate more.

Avoid Sidetracking the Meeting

Avoid talking to your neighbor or going off on a tangent about something unrelated. Stick to the subject at hand. The sooner you complete the agenda, the sooner the meeting will end.

ETIQUETTE DILEMMA

Q. *Should a man stand when a woman enters or leaves the room?*

A. *While chivalry is a lovely practice socially, in the business world treating women differently from men is considered sexist, and should not be practiced. Treat men and women equally in the business world. While your intention when standing is to show respect for women, if you wouldn't stand when a man enters or leaves a room in the workplace, don't do it for a woman.*

Be Careful Not to Interrupt

Let others make their points, then speak. If you need to, raise your hand to get the chairperson's permission to speak.

Don't Dominate the Meeting

Speak only if you have something meaningful to add to the discussion.

Avoid Looking at Your Phone

In this 24/7, always-connected world, you might have a hard time not texting or reading email on your smartphone while in a meeting. However, not only is using your phone disrespectful, looking at it keeps you from being a contributing participant. Put the phone away and stay focused.

I spoke to a Rotary group that collected dollar bills from members who were guilty of bad behavior. One of the transgressions was

ETIQUETTE DILEMMA

Q. *What do I do when someone keeps talking to me during the meeting about unrelated topics or makes side comments?*

A. *Having someone talk to you during the meeting is always frustrating. Not only does it reflect poorly on the other person, participating in side conversation will make you look unprofessional as well. If the talker is sitting next to you, suggest that you talk after the meeting, and state that right now you want to be sure you don't miss what's being discussed. If this person is farther away, put your finger to your lips and move your eyes toward the speaker to indicate you'd like to listen.*

texting or emailing during the meeting. I thought this was a great idea. You could make a no-phone-use policy in your company meetings, and then donate the money to a local charity.

TELECONFERENCE MANNERS

Teleconferences have allowed us to include people in other locations, and this can speed up projects and decisions. But, for a variety of reasons, teleconferences can be a more challenging way to conduct meetings. Practicing some conference call etiquette will make them more productive and useful for everyone, especially those participating from other offices.

Have a Facilitator

A meeting facilitator is essential to manage the conference call and make sure everyone is included.

The facilitator or person organizing the meeting should ensure the participants have the call-in number and the participant code a few days before the meeting. Include the number and participant code on the agenda and in the meeting invitation. Send a reminder an hour before the call. And make sure the conference phone is working before the meeting. Check in with those on the line to confirm they can hear what is being said.

Those calling in should allot time before the meeting starts to call the conference line and ensure the conference phone is working.

Heed the Mute Button

When you're calling into a meeting, always put your phone on mute when you're not talking. Often headsets or even the handset held close to your mouth will lead to you sounding like Darth Vader breathing over the line, which is annoying to those listening in. If your phone doesn't have a mute button, press *6 to mute yourself and then press it again to unmute yourself. Always mute your phone if you are typing or calling from a noisy background.

It is considerate for the facilitator and those in remote offices to mute the phone in the meeting room while people assemble or if there is a noisy activity such as distributing a handout. Let those calling in know that you are going to mute the phone during this time.

Make Introductions

Once the meeting has started and the majority of the participants have called in, the facilitator's role is to welcome everyone and make or facilitate introductions. The best way to approach introductions is to have those in the meeting room take turns stating their name and title or reason for being in the meeting. The facilitator can then call on the remote offices one by one. Example: "Let's have those folks calling in from the Denver office introduce themselves. ... Great, thank you Denver. I know we have Barb on the line from San Francisco. Barb, please introduce yourself."

Call on the Remote Employees

Once everyone has introduced themselves and the meeting is underway, the facilitator is responsible for regularly asking those calling in for their opinion or feedback. For those dialing in from an outside office, it can be hard to interrupt a bigger group so they may be less likely to do so. Think of the remote folks as introverts. They may have information to add to the discussion, but they're not as likely to offer their opinion without being prompted.

Rather than asking, "Does anyone on the phone have something to add?" call on individuals or invite people by location to share their thoughts. When you do call on a remote group by location—"Folks in San Francisco, anything to add?"—give them extra time to unmute the phone and to decide who in the room is going to speak.

Avoid Side Conversations

When people have side conversations, those who have dialed in will have a difficult time hearing what's being shared. They usually won't know if what they hear is a side conversation or the topic being discussed. The facilitator should stop side conversations and ensure one person speaks at a time so that everyone can hear the discussion.

Be Mindful of Noise

When you're on a conference call and someone shuffles paper or drags a coffee cup across the table next to the speakerphone it sounds like a thunderstorm. Be aware of how simple things like passing paper, pulling a chair in or clicking a pen are amplified by the speakerphone and sound a lot louder to those listening in.

The facilitator can remind those attending the meeting at the beginning to be mindful of noise they are making, so those calling in are not overwhelmed with loud noises. If someone is making unintentional noise during the meeting, the facilitator needs to ask again that people be mindful of the noise they are making and also to ask remote attendees to mute their phones when not speaking.

Imagine Those Calling In Are in The Room

As a participant in the main meeting room, you might inadvertently forget your colleagues on the phone. Use any of these tactics to help you remember they are on the call:

- Put name placards with their names on the table or write their names on a whiteboard.

- Have laminated photos of remote employees created that you hang up or tape to empty chairs before the meeting starts.

- If you have video capability, use it so that you can see those calling in and they can see you.

Please Disconnect

When the meeting or discussion with those on the line is over, be sure to completely hang up the phone. In one of my corporate jobs some of my coworkers partnered with a few outside organizations on a project. My colleagues shared that the folks from one group were particularly uncooperative and disorganized. After a frustrating meeting ended, the chair started complaining about how difficult the people from this organization were to work with. Others in the room joined in and shared their frustrations as well. This went on for some time until eventually, a fellow coworker who had called in and was still on the line reminded everyone that the line was live.

ETIQUETTE DILEMMA

Q. *Someone on the conference call is a heavy breather. Can we do anything about that?*

A. *If the facilitator doesn't say anything, go ahead and speak up. Say, "I'd like to remind people to mute their phones when they aren't talking. We're getting a lot of noise from those on the line." No one will be embarrassed because you're addressing the whole group.*

Thank goodness the outside group had hung up—it could have been disastrous!

Additional ways you can make your teleconferences more productive and useful:

- State your first and last name when you call in.

- Be careful not to interrupt others. Wait until they are finished before you step in.

- Don't multitask when you're on a call, as this will keep you from focusing on the meeting. Be present and pay attention.

- Avoid calling from noisy places. People will hear the background noise making it hard to hear you and others.

- Don't mistake the hold button for the mute button. If you select the hold button, you may subject the callers to hold music, thereby interrupting the meeting with strains of Kenny G.

- Don't eat or drink while on the call.

- Don't leave the call early. Wait until the facilitator has ended the meeting.

Meeting mayhem can slow down your company. Having fewer meetings, and meetings that are more focused and productive with the right people in the room, will lead to a healthier bottom line and happier employees. A win-win for everyone!

CHAPTER SEVEN

YIKES! MY BOSS SENT ME A FRIEND REQUEST

Digital Diplomacy

A colleague of mine told me that in one of his former jobs he and his coworker, Bill, were called into their boss's office. The boss called a client using the speakerphone and didn't tell the client there were others in the room. When the boss mentioned something Bill was working on, the client said, "Oh, Bill, that son of a $%&#@." As my colleague said, "Tense moment."

....

L ooking back in old etiquette books, I marvel at how much communication etiquette has changed. Then, it was focused on landlines with rotary dials, letters and in-person communication. Today, with smartphones, speakerphones, email, voicemail, instant messaging and social media, communication etiquette has gotten much more complicated.

According to the most recent report by Nielsen, Americans spend sixty hours a week on digital devices.[1] Without body language and, oftentimes, tone, we have a harder time communicating our meaning, and we can forget there is a real person receiving our message.

When talking to someone face to face, place priority on the person in front of you as opposed to whatever digital tool you're using—landline, smartphone, tablet or computer. It's disrespectful to answer your phone or send a text when you are meeting face to face with someone. Doing so would be similar to turning your back on the person and forcing him to stare at it while you talk to the person across the room.

In one of my company's teen manners classes, the teacher asked one of the teens a question and then pulled out her smartphone and pretended to text someone. The teen was gobsmacked. He stuttered and looked confused and hurt. She pointed out that that is what it feels like when you focus on your phone rather than the person you are with. The teens got the message loud and clear.

Each digital tool has specific etiquette guidelines. Let's start with email.

EMAIL ETIQUETTE

I received an email from my doctor's office with the email addresses of all her patients in the "To" field. Oops! Let's look at why this was a problem. To begin with, having all of the email addresses in the "To" field meant the header was very long, so I had to scroll down quite a ways before I got to the email message. Additionally, everyone on the email could see all the personal email addresses of the doctor's patients. This also meant the receivers could click "Reply All" and send a message to everyone on the list—which one of the patients did. And what he said was quite inflammatory about the doctor.

Additionally, because this was a doctor's office, allowing everyone to see the email addresses of the other patients was a violation of the Health Insurance Portability and Accountability Act (HIPAA), a serious infraction. The person who sent the email probably had no idea she needed to put a group of patients' email addresses in the "BCC"⋆ field to protect the privacy of the recipients.

Doctors' employees are not the only ones who need to be concerned about privacy issues; you must protect the privacy of your contacts if they don't know each other. When there are more than a few email addresses, always put them in the BCC field, unless for some reason everyone should see who was addressed in the email and they all know each other.

Be an email pro by paying attention to these additional email etiquette tips:

Keep Your Emails Brief and to the Point

We are inundated with hundreds of emails every day, and if you hope to have people read your email messages, you must keep them short.

Consider What You're Trying to Communicate

Make your topic clear both in the subject line and in the first part of the email. Let's say you want someone to review a document by a certain date. State in the subject line something like: "Please review June newsletter by noon on April 25." Your first sentence should reiterate the subject line.

Use bullet points to make the content easier to read and absorb. Stick to one subject per email. I also like to organize the email with subheads so that if the recipient scans the email, she can read and understand it more easily. Here's an example:

⋆BCC stands for blind carbon copy. When putting an email address in the BCC field, the sender conceals the addressee's identity and address.

Sample Email

....

To: Marketing Senior Vice President

From: Marketing Director

Subject: Second-quarter marketing report

Hi Sarah,

I have attached the quarterly marketing report for the board meeting. Here are the highlights:

Events

- 225 people attended our Bellevue shred-a-thon in April. This is 38% more than last year.

Campaigns

- The auto-loan campaign resulted in 78 new loans and 19 refinances from other financial institutions. This exceeded our goal of 65 new loans and 15 refinances.

- 194 customers opted in to the skip-a-payment campaign. This is down slightly from 206 opt-ins in the second quarter last year.

Staffing

- We hired a social media coordinator who started May 25. Heather is already increasing traffic and followers on our social media sites.

Please let me know if you have any questions.

Best regards,

Jay

....

Use "EOM"

When you have a very short message to send, put it in the subject line, such as, "See you at Salty's at noon" and add EOM at the end, which stands for End of Message. That says to the recipient that nothing is in the body of the email; instead, the complete message is in the subject line.

You will have to educate people about what EOM means before using it, but it sure saves people time opening and reading emails.

Never Leave Your Subject Line Blank

Not having a subject line is like not having a title on the cover of a book. Your subject line needs to accurately and briefly state what the email is about.

I know someone who puts only his name in the subject line. Not only does it not give me any clue as to what the email is about, it seems a bit self-important. Please don't do this.

Update the Subject Line

If the email has been forwarded and no longer speaks to the subject line, be sure to change it to reflect the new content in the email. Better yet, remove the old content or start a new email so the person reading it doesn't have to wade through irrelevant information.

Have a Greeting and Closing

One of the most common email etiquette blunders is not having a greeting and a closing. Skipping those items is like not saying hello or goodbye to someone you meet in person. However, if you're sending several emails back and forth to the same person, you can dispense with a greeting and closing every time.

That brings me to another point: If an email exchange has gone back and forth more than three times, it's time to pick up the phone or stop by the person's office and have a discussion. You'll resolve the issue much faster and with more clarity.

Be Careful about Using "Reply All"

Consider who really needs to see your response to an email. Often it's just the person who sent the email. Receiving unnecessary emails from Reply All is one of the biggest irritants I hear from my clients.

In one of my corporate jobs an email was sent that didn't apply to most of the people on the email. I'm not quite sure why we were included. But many of those people used Reply All to ask to be taken off the distribution list. Which meant not only were we getting an unnecessary email, we were being inundated with additional emails of people asking to be taken off the email list. It was maddening!

ETIQUETTE DILEMMA

Q. *I want to know if my emails are being received and read. Is it okay to use the sent receipt option?*

A. *Unless you have a legal reason to track whether your email has been received, the sent receipt option is usually annoying to people; it can appear as if you are stalking them. Send your email, and if you don't get a response within a few days, follow up in another email or pick up the phone and call the person.*

Include a Signature

Make sure your emails have a professional signature that includes your full name, company name, contact information and maybe your company website.

Proof Your Emails

Before you send your emails, take a moment to read them. I'm always amazed at how many mistakes I catch when I take the time to do this.

A few more email tips:

- Use your out-of-office auto responder when you are away for more than a day.

- Don't use all upper case in any medium. IT MAKES IT LOOK AS IF YOU ARE SHOUTING!

- Avoid using email when you should use the phone. Call or meet with the recipient in person if the information you're conveying is confidential, complicated, sensitive or likely to be difficult news to receive.

- Nix using the urgent symbol on a regular basis. Because many people overuse the tool, it is usually not effective in getting your emails read quicker. If your message is truly time sensitive, it's best to call or visit the recipient.

- Don't email or respond when you're emotional. You'll regret it. Give yourself time to calm down and then ask yourself if the email is really warranted or if the information should be communicated in person.

PHONE ETIQUETTE

According to studies conducted by BI Intelligence, one in every five people throughout the world has a smartphone.[2] In the

United States, 64 percent of the population has a smartphone and the numbers continue to grow, according to research by Pew Research Center.[3] That's a lot of talking, texting, emailing and web surfing! Is it any wonder people are getting more comfortable with their phones and less so with other people?

Stash that Phone

As I mentioned before, it's respectful to put your phone away and give the people in front of you your full attention. To avoid the temptation of looking at your phone when it lights up or rings, turn the ringer off and put it away when you meet with others.

Please don't put your phone on the table in a meeting. It signals that the phone is more important than the people in front of you, and it only adds to the temptation to pick it up when it lights up with a text or email. Trust me, I know this. Every time

---

ETIQUETTE DILEMMA

Q. *I don't wear a watch, so I use my smartphone to check the time. If I'm meeting with another person, is it okay to look at my phone for the time?*

A. *I encourage you to wear a watch because it's much easier to look at it surreptitiously than your smartphone, and the action is less distracting. If you wear a smartwatch in meetings, be sure to turn the notifications off. However, if a watch is just not your style, state at the start of the meeting that you want to be mindful of the time and that you use your phone to check the time. Before you do look at it, say, "Let me see what time it is. Excuse me." Many meeting rooms have clocks. If that's the case, all of this is a moot point. Look at the clock to check the time.*

I sit down to dinner with my husband and have forgotten to stash my phone, the moment it dings or lights up, I look at it. Shame on me!

Alert Others

When you are expecting an important call or message, let those you're meeting with know in advance. Put your phone on vibrate in your pocket or on your lap so that if you receive a call, you'll feel it but won't disturb others. You will need to look at your phone when it vibrates. If the expected call comes in, excuse yourself and take it outside.

More phone do's and don'ts:

Keep your voice down. Also, avoid talking in public places where you will disturb others.

Respect servers. When interacting with folks serving you— the barista, sales clerk, bank teller, etc.—put your phone away and give the person your full attention.

Smile. A smile puts warmth in your voice. Without body language to communicate meaning, having a friendly tone on the phone is even more important.

End offline conversations. Before answering the phone, end any conversation you are having. Continuing to talk with someone in person as you answer the phone, but before you say hello, is annoying and disrespectful to the caller.

Don't interrupt. Try not to interrupt or rush a caller. Let him finish what he has to say before you speak.

Ask permission. Always ask permission before putting someone on hold. When you ask, "May I put you on hold?" rather than saying, "Please hold," you allow the caller to opt in, and you'll sound more gracious.

Priority rules. If someone stops by your desk when you're on the phone, the person on the phone gets priority. If you're meeting with someone and your phone rings, the person in front of you gets priority. Don't answer the phone unless you had a phone meeting scheduled. In that case, you would explain to the person visiting you that you were expecting the call and need to take it. Be sure to follow up with the visitor later.

Don't eat. It's not pleasant hearing someone chew in your ear on the phone.

Mind the background noise. Before you talk on the phone, take reasonable precautions that you aren't interrupted in some way by a barking dog, espresso machine or other distracting noise.

Speakerphones

Speakerphones are for conference calls or meetings with many people in one room. It is rare a person would need to put a caller on speakerphone when only two people are conversing. Speakerphones can also make conversations harder to hear, and might make you seem as if you are too busy or too important

ETIQUETTE DILEMMA

Q. *Who calls back when a call is dropped? I find that when a call is dropped, either both parties call back at the same time and both calls go to voicemail, or neither calls back and each waits for the other person to call.*

A. *Let me end the madness. The person who placed the call is the person who calls back. If Susie Q calls you and the connection is lost, you may sit tight and let Ms. Q ring you back.*

to hold the phone. However, if you must put a caller on speaker, always ask permission before doing so.

If you put someone on speakerphone, make sure you're not disturbing anyone around you and that the person on the line can hear you clearly. For all of these reasons, use them sparingly.

INSTANT MESSAGE AND TEXTING ETIQUETTE

Instant messaging and texts are great for quick, easy-to-answer topics. But neither is appropriate for more formal or lengthy discussions. Keep these tips in mind:

Ask Before Chatting

Before sending an instant message, ask first if someone can chat. Never send a message when you know someone is in a meeting or is unavailable.

Keep It Brief

Before you send a message, make sure it's the right medium. Instant and text messages are appropriate for brief messages that don't require a lengthy reply or aren't confidential. If your message is more than a couple of sentences, use email or the phone.

ETIQUETTE DILEMMA

Q. *I received a text from someone who isn't in my contacts list, and the person didn't state his or her name, so I don't know who it is. How do I respond?*

A. *Simply respond by saying, "I'm sorry, I don't recognize this number; can you tell me who this is?"*

Mind the Message

Because instant messages pop up on someone's computer, they are less private. Your recipient might be meeting with another person when the message appears on her computer, allowing her guest to see it. Never send anything you wouldn't want others to see. And don't deliver bad news in messages, just as you wouldn't in email.

Spelling and Grammar Count

Watch your spelling. You might think that because instant messages and texts are more casual and immediate, spelling errors or text-speak is acceptable. However, spelling and proper grammar are still important in business communication. Be careful, too, to proof what you write before you send it. Smartphones often insert incorrect words if you're not paying attention. Professional writing will reflect more positively on you.

Set Your Status

When you aren't available, use your away-message alerts. Instant messaging is a more immediate medium, so if your status shows you're available people will wonder why you aren't responding.

ETIQUETTE DILEMMA

Q. *A client texts me after hours and on weekends. Do I need to respond right away?*

A. *No, you don't. You have to decide when you want to be "on the clock" and when you're on personal time. It's okay to set some boundaries. You can share your typical work hours and explain to your client that you usually don't work outside of those hours so that you can focus on your personal life.*

That said, when you are messaging others, don't expect them to drop everything to respond to your instant messages. We are all busy and should not be expected to be at the beck and call of others.

VOICEMAIL ETIQUETTE

Your voicemail messages will be more polished and effective if you follow these tips:

- Practice what you're going to say before you leave a voicemail message and before you create your own voicemail greeting or away message.

- Keep your messages brief. If what you have to say is lengthy just state, "Please call me so that we can discuss the xyz project."

- Always identify who you are and your company. State both your first and last name even if you think the person knows who you are.

- Include the best time to call you back or state when you will call back. When calling clients, typically you would call back rather than ask the client to call you, unless you're returning a call.

- Speak slowly, especially when you state your phone number. Mention your name and phone number at the beginning and end of the message.

- For your own voicemail greeting, keep your message current and up to date. If you will be out of the office for more than a day, create an out-of-office message. Make a tickler note to remind yourself to turn it off when you return.

SOCIAL MEDIA ETIQUETTE

Social media use has exploded over the last several years, and more and more people are using it for business. Blogs, Facebook, LinkedIn, Instagram, Twitter, Pinterest, YouTube and more are invaluable tools for making social and business connections online. To succeed with social media, learn the "rules of engagement" before you jump in and accidentally alienate your followers, friends or contacts.

The following etiquette points apply to all social media:

Don't Spam

If you are using social media to promote your business or generate contacts, do not spam your connections. That is, don't send repeated updates about your business, product or book. It would be like someone walking into a cocktail party and screaming to everyone he sees, "Buy my product!" How annoying is that?

Be Professional and Courteous

Remember, everything you say on any online site is in cyberspace forever. And people are looking at what you say—potential and current employers, college admissions staff, potential landlords, clients, you name it. So hold the swear words, avoid the political and religious rants, be courteous and don't criticize anyone even if she is being a jerk.

Before you post something, ask yourself is it nice, is it necessary, do I want my boss or parents to see it, do I want it on the home page of the local paper? If your answer is no to any of those questions, don't post it.

If you are responsible for posting content on a company Facebook page, LinkedIn page or Twitter feed, be especially mindful of posting controversial topics. As a representative of the company, post only topics, content and positive messages that represent the company's views.

Engage with Your Followers

Social media is all about building relationships with people. Think of your communication online as a dialogue rather than a monologue. Take time to interact with your followers. Comment on their posts and retweet or share any posts you think are interesting or valuable. However, be careful not to randomly share posts that don't have much value, as your connections may find it annoying or silly, which probably won't have the effect you desire.

Say "Thank You"

Thank people for recommendations, introductions, referrals and shares. When you say "thank you," people are more willing to help you.

Don't Overshare

Unless you're incredibly clever, regularly posting mundane things like what you had for lunch or a bunch of photos of your "cute" kids gets really old for your followers. Don't feel compelled to share everything you're doing; wait until it's interesting, meaningful or helpful.

You'll encounter people who share every thought and action no matter how personal—"Going to the doctor for my colonoscopy." Please don't do this. Have some boundaries. If you wouldn't say it in person to someone you don't know very well, assume it won't be well received on social media. Lastly, be mindful of how often you post. Even if what you have to say is interesting, if you're filling up someone's wall or feed they will probably hide, unfriend or unfollow you.

TWITTER

Twitter has been described as a mini-blog. Users have 140 characters to update their followers about anything and everything. When you follow someone you see their updates, and when someone follows you they see your updates. You can use the Twitter search function to search topics, words or people you'd like to follow.

Take time on Twitter to observe first. Hold off on tweeting (posting) until you understand the lay of the land. Watch the public timeline, which is all Twitter users' posts at any one time, to see what people are talking about. Or look at the trending topics which show up on the left side of twitter.com. Those are the words or phrases that are showing up the most in tweets (posts).

PORTABLE AUDIO PLAYER ETIQUETTE

If you work in a job that allows you to listen to music on a portable player, your coworkers will thank you for practicing these guidelines:

• *Remove both ear-buds when someone is talking to you. If you remove just one it looks as if you're giving the person in front of you half of your attention.*

• *Keep the volume down so that others can't hear your music.*

• *Never wear ear-buds in a communal place. Be engaged and attentive to the people around you.*

• *Don't sing and bop. Even if you're a great singer, the workplace is not the place to get your groove on.*

Create a Profile

Be sure to set up a Twitter profile with at least a bio and photo (also called an avatar). Humanize your profile so people know who you are—that will help them decide if they want to follow you. Choose what interests you want to highlight to tweet about, and then start tweeting. I always look at someone's bio and tweets to see if we have anything in common before I agree to follow them. No bio? No avatar? No follow.

Build Relationships, Not Just Followers

There are plenty of tools out there that allow you to build your follower base with little effort, so that you can go from zero to two thousand followers in a couple of days. Don't do it! People want to engage with others who share similar interests, not with stalkers who just want to promote their products or artificially inflate their follower numbers. Build relationships with a smaller number of followers, based on mutual interests.

The 80 Percent/20 Percent Rule

When posting for your company, only 20 percent of your tweets should be about your business, product, event or book. The remaining 80 percent of your tweets should be informative, helpful, interesting or of a personal nature—posts that allow others to get to know you and are useful to them.

Acknowledge Retweets

When people retweet you, thank them in a direct message, or publicly thank a group of people who have retweeted you. This keeps you from cluttering up the news feed with a bunch of individual thank-you posts.

#FollowFriday

Friday is the day Twitter users recognize their most interesting, clever, helpful or fun followers by naming them and writing #FF for FollowFriday. You can state why they are worthy of following. When people like and feel connected to you, they will most likely #FF you, too.

Direct Message (DM) Personal Messages

If you have a personal conversation with one person, change it to a direct message so that you're not filling up the Twitter feed with a personal dialogue. Think of it as being at a party. If you were talking directly to one person about something that does not relate to others at the party, you'd probably speak quietly so just that person could hear you.

ETIQUETTE DILEMMA

Q. *Someone I don't recognize sent me a LinkedIn connection request, and she used the default message so I don't have any sense of how I might know her. It's possible we've met and that I can't remember meeting. Should I ignore the request and risk insulting her, or should I just accept the request?*

A. *When meeting a lot of people, forgetting if you know someone is pretty commonplace. Send a message to the person without accepting the request, and write something along the lines of, "Hello Donna, forgive my poor memory, but can you remind me where we met?" If you haven't met, hopefully Donna will respond and be upfront about it. If you have met, she will most likely state how you know each other. If you get no response, you can assume it was someone you don't know.*

LINKEDIN

Many people view LinkedIn as a site for job seekers and recruiters, but it is so much more. LinkedIn is a wonderful site to get professional advice, stay in touch with your colleagues and share industry best practices and resources.

LinkedIn is like your virtual resume and rolodex. It's a place to list your work history, qualifications, skills and recommendations.

You can connect with people you have worked with or met at networking events and who you want to stay in touch with on a professional level. These folks extend your network and can introduce you to others who may be helpful in your career, business or job search.

Follow these etiquette guidelines to stay in the good graces of your connections:

Your Photo Matters

Post a professional-looking headshot on your profile. Avoid an image of you and your kids or your friends or anything that is blurry or hard to see. Your image will be seen by recruiters, clients, colleagues, partners or associates, and hiring managers, so make sure it reflects well on you.

Don't Default

Personalize your connection requests so that people know who you are and where you met. When requesting to connect, avoid using the default message that LinkedIn provides. In order to personalize the message, go to the person's profile and click on "Connect." You can then choose one of the options for how you know this person and write a personalized note.

Personalizing your request is also a terrific way to increase your visibility and make a connection with someone. Many people will not connect with those who haven't taken the time to personalize the request, especially if it's someone the person doesn't know. Equally important: Write your own message for recommendation requests, rather than using the LinkedIn default message.

Do I Know You?

Avoid asking someone you haven't met to connect with you, and don't connect with someone you don't know or who you don't respect. Once connected, that person could ask you to make an introduction or request a recommendation. If you don't know or feel good about him, you're risking your professional reputation by making the introduction or recommendation. You can click the "X" so as not to connect with this person; he or she will not get a message that you declined the connection request.

Stick to Work Topics

What you post in your updates should be of a professional nature, such as a project you're working on, a conference you're attending or an interesting article you read.

If you make comments in group discussions, be respectful even if you disagree with someone. Never tell someone they are wrong. Leave people thinking what a gracious, kind person you are even when others around you are being rude or nasty.

FACEBOOK

Facebook was created as a social-networking site for college students and has become the site that is searched more than Google with nearly 1.5 billion active users.[4] When both grandparents and grandkids are on Facebook, you know it is a site that can't be ignored.

Practice these tips to be a good friend and connection on Facebook:

Watch Who You "Friend"

Facebook is like your house. You wouldn't invite everyone into your house and you don't need to do it on Facebook. Be thoughtful about who you want to friend. Once you say yes to someone from a particular group, you may find it hard to ignore a request from someone else from that group. Also, never connect with your boss or clients. While you may be squeaky clean on the site, your friends may say or do things that reflect badly on you. It's just not worth the risk.

Groups Are For Groups

Never form a group for your business. Groups are for people who share a similar interest, passion, hobby or sport. If you want to have a company presence on Facebook, create a company page.

ETIQUETTE DILEMMA

Q. *My boss sent me a Facebook friend request, but I'm really uncomfortable with having him as a Facebook friend. What do I do?*

A. *If someone like your boss, client or coworker sends a friend request, invite him to connect with you on LinkedIn instead. If you feel you must have an explanation, simply say, "I limit my Facebook connections to a small group of my close friends and family, but I would love to connect with you on LinkedIn."*

Tag Lightly

Don't post or tag your coworkers or friends in photos or videos without their permission, especially ones that could be embarrassing to them.

No Spam

If you'd like to share company information, events or products, create a company page and share business-related information there. Your friends will thank you. And, as on Twitter, the same 80 percent/20 percent rule applies. Eighty percent of your posts should include interesting facts, helpful tips, articles and videos. Only 20 percent of your posts should be promotional in nature.

Never post promotional messages on someone else's Facebook page. This is a very big no-no. Doing so could be compared to getting on stage at a presentation, grabbing the microphone from the speaker and telling the audience that they should buy your product.

Be Helpful

I encourage you to "like" pages of companies you enjoy. If you are a business owner or you post for your company, take time to

ETIQUETTE DILEMMA

Q. *My colleague posted a photo that is really not flattering of me. Should I say something or just let it go?*

A. *You have every right to ask that it be removed. Explain to your colleague that you're not comfortable with people seeing that photo of you and ask her if she would please remove it.*

comment on other company pages and share interesting content they have posted, on your own page. Focus on being helpful and letting your followers know about companies and content you think are interesting. People will appreciate your interest and will be more likely to post about your company or content.

Our world has changed considerably with the advances in technology. I remember when a cell phone was as big as a brick and had an antenna as thick as a slim cigar. Technology has come a long way since then. What hasn't changed is the importance of being courteous and respectful of others, no matter what device or site you're using.

CHAPTER EIGHT

TWO KISSES OR ONE?

Travel Etiquette in a Global World

My sister-in-law, Beth, who lives in Australia, was flying home in the evening from an interstate business trip. When her flight was called, she left the comfort of the lounge only to be told at the gate that the flight would be delayed by thirty minutes.

The young man standing next to her let out a sigh, and she thought he was going to exchange some angry words with the ground staff. Instead, he turned to Beth and said, "Might as well make the most of it. My name's Jack, I've been traveling since six this morning and I'm bushed. Who are you, and what's your story?"

Beth smiled and struck up a conversation with the young man. He shared with her that he would like to get into marketing someday. So they exchanged email addresses, and Beth invited him to contact her if and when he needed help in getting started.

She shared, "He was a wonderful young man who made the most of thirty minutes of frustration by connecting with another human being. I hope he gets in touch."

....

Traveling for business is an exciting prospect: You get to go to places you may not have seen; sometimes stay in luxury hotels; and you don't have to foot the bill. But don't confuse this with vacation travel. When you are traveling for business, whether to attend a convention or meet with a client, you are representing not just yourself, but your company as well. Your actions and how you present yourself are a reflection of the company you work for—from how you're dressed, to how you treat people, to your professional demeanor. You may also encounter cultural differences that are stressful or frustrating.

Being aware of how to present yourself and learning how to navigate tipping and cultural nuances will make your travel more enjoyable and effective.

TRAVEL ATTIRE

While you may be tempted to wear your comfortable sweats or broken-in jeans while traveling, business casual attire is more appropriate for a few reasons. If your luggage is lost and you have to go straight to a meeting, you'll be much more comfortable if you're dressed appropriately. You also never know who you will meet on your travels. A potential client or VIP could be sitting next to

A WORD ABOUT PER DIEM

If you have to travel overnight for work, most companies will give you a per diem (Latin for "per day"), an allotted amount you're allowed to spend on food each day. Before you go crazy ordering lobster and bottles of Dom Pérignon at dinner, find out if there is a specified amount per meal and if alcoholic beverages are included. Even if you have an unlimited amount to spend on food, don't take that as an invitation to spend foolishly. When you hand in your receipts, your boss may not think highly of your extravagant spending, which could affect being selected for future trips or a promotion. Spend the company money as if it were your own money.

you. You'll make a better impression and feel more confident if you are dressed well. You'll also be taken more seriously.

BE PREPARED

If you are flying more than a couple of hours to your destination, plan to arrive the day before your meeting or presentation. That way if there are any flight delays you won't risk missing your meeting.

Arrive at the airport two hours before your flight. You will have ample time to check in, get through security and arrive at your gate without needing to rush. I learned this the hard way. I had a tendency to arrive about an hour before my flight, and one time I missed my plane to a client presentation across the country. Thankfully, I was able to get on a later flight, but I arrived very late that night because I missed the connecting flight. Needless to say, the situation was quite stressful. Thank goodness my presentation was the next day. Now I make a

ETIQUETTE DILEMMA

Q. *What do I do if I'm seated next to a family with a screaming child throughout the flight?*

A. *If the plane is not full, you could ask the flight attendant if he would seat you in another area. If you're not able to move, put on headphones and try to tune out the noise. However, if the child is screaming and carrying on because of negligent parents, get up and speak to a flight attendant and ask him if he could talk to the parents. Do not try to speak to the parents yourself. You'll most likely just escalate the situation.*

point of always arriving two hours before my flight leaves, so that this never happens again.

Be sure you have your itinerary with you, including phone numbers of the hotel you're staying in, the limo or rental car company, your company host, etc. If you're delayed, you can inform those who are counting on your arrival at a certain time.

I encourage you to give your hosts your itinerary information—your flight information (airline, flight number and arrival time), your hotel and your cell phone number, so that they know when to expect you and where to find you.

ETIQUETTE DILEMMA

Q. *I have long legs, and I really dislike it when the person sitting in front of me reclines his seat. I lose my leg room and it makes eating more difficult at meal time. Should I get one of those gadgets to keep people from reclining their seats into my knees?*

A. *As airlines have decreased the amount of legroom space, you might be tempted to take matters into your own hands. However, preventing someone from reclining his seat is not kind. If you are eating, politely ask the person in front of you if he would mind waiting to recline until you are finished with your meal. If the reclining seat is indeed hitting your long legs, you could nicely explain the seat is hurting your knees and would he mind decreasing the amount he is reclining his seat. I can't guarantee people will respond favorably, but asking politely is much better than rudely forcing the issue with a gadget that keeps the person from reclining. Remember, reclining your seat is your right as well. Would you want someone to prevent you from reclining your seat?*

Carry enough cash to cover tips for the driver or taxi and hotel staff. *(See Tipping Etiquette later in this chapter.)*

AIRPLANE ETIQUETTE

When booking your ticket, be mindful of what kind of traveler you are. If you like to sleep while flying, reserve the window seat so people don't have to wake you or crawl over you to get out. If you have long legs or tend to get up a lot during a flight, ask for an aisle seat. And if you're stuck with the dreaded middle seat, you'll be happy to know you get to use both armrests on either side of your seat.

Be Helpful

If you see someone struggling to put her luggage in the overhead compartment, offer to help. And, if someone helps you with your luggage, be sure to say thank you.

ETIQUETTE DILEMMA

Q. *I prefer relaxing when I'm flying and not talking to my seatmate. Is there a polite way to let him know I don't want to talk?*

A. *Simply say "I'd love to talk but I really need to focus on a work project" (or "catch up on my reading" or "sleep"). If you are someone who likes to talk with your seatmate, test the waters by asking an innocuous question like, "Are you traveling for business or pleasure?" If the answer is curt, you'll know conversation is not in the cards.*

Avoid the Seat-Yank

When you need to get in and out of your seat, be mindful of not pulling on the seat in front of you. I'm sure you don't want to give someone whiplash when you stand up or sit down.

Be Courteous

Be nice to the flight attendants. They have a hard job and are not your personal servants. You'll receive better service if you are courteous to them.

Recline with Caution

If you wish to recline your seat, you might warn the person behind you before doing so. Then recline slowly. When meals are served, be considerate of the person behind you by putting your seatback up so that she can eat without having your chair in her face.

Electronic Device Diplomacy

When listening to music or watching a movie on your digital

AIRPLANE TIPS

- *Keep the shade closed if people are watching a movie.*
- *Don't take your socks off. Eau-de-sweaty-feet is not anyone's choice of scent.*
- *Don't take care of any personal hygiene at your seat—clipping or painting your nails, flossing your teeth, shaving or putting on makeup. Use the bathroom to do these things.*
- *Keep the alcohol consumption at a minimum. Remember, this is business travel.*

device, use earbuds so that the noise doesn't bother those around you. Also, be careful of your movie selection. Intentionally or not, your seatmates will see what you are viewing, so what's showing on your screen should not be any racier than an R-rated film. And, if children are sitting next to you, be extra cautious about what you're viewing. Be vigilant too about not showing confidential company information on your laptop or tablet. You never know who might be viewing your screen. You can purchase a screen guard which prevents your information from being viewed from the side.

Disembark in Order

Be mindful that the system for disembarking the plane is row by row. As people get out of their seats and move into the aisle, give them space and time to get their luggage out of the overhead compartment. Put your patience hat on while you wait your turn to disembark. I promise two extra minutes will not kill you.

ON THE ROAD

Driving to a meeting with a coworker or boss is a good time to get to know your colleague better. Take advantage of this time to learn about your road buddy rather than focusing on work or personal matters.

Clean Your Ride

If you drive in your car, be sure it's clean and not filled with garbage and papers. Think about the impression you're making.

Mood Music

If you want to listen to the radio, ask your passenger first if he minds. Keep the volume low so that you can still carry on a conversation. Your music selection should be PG rated—avoid anything that is really jarring or has offensive lyrics. Ask your passenger if the music selection is acceptable to him.

Seating Matters

When you are driving with a few people, give the most-honored person—your boss or client—the front passenger seat. If you're riding in a van, let the older and the more senior folks sit towards the front so they don't have to climb into the back.

Silence Can Be Golden

Be aware of your passenger's interest in talking. If she is being quiet and not engaging much in the conversation, assume she doesn't want to converse. This would be a good time to put the radio on quietly.

When I'm traveling with someone, I enjoy chatting for a while, and then I like to watch the scenery or read a book and then maybe come back to a conversation a little later. It allows my introverted energy a chance to recharge. Years ago, I took a business trip on a train with a talkative coworker who wanted to chat the whole three hours we were traveling. Despite my efforts to end the conversation and try to read my book, she kept talking. While she's a delightful person, I was exhausted at the end of that train ride.

Stash the Phone

If you are the passenger, stay present with the driver at least in the beginning of your journey. If you need to check email or text for work reasons, ask first if the driver minds if you do so. Then keep it brief. Never answer the phone or call someone while in the car with another person. Your traveling companion will be uncomfortable having to listen to your conversation.

TRAINS

Commuting by train has become a nice alternative to driving. Many train stations have been renovated and train cars are much more comfortable than they once were. A lot of the rules that apply to airplane travel also apply to train travel.

- Wear headphones when listening to music or a video.

- Before opening or closing the shade, ask the person sitting next to you if he minds.

- Put garbage in the trash receptacles, not the seat pocket.

- Because cell phone use is allowed on trains, be especially mindful of talking on the phone around others. Most people do not enjoy hearing someone converse on the phone near them.

- Talk in a more private area rather than at your seat and keep your calls short. Never discuss personal, confidential or business information where others might hear your conversation.

....

TAXI-SEATING TIP

When traveling in a taxi with your boss or a client, the best seat is the backseat closest to the curb. It is polite to get in first, slide across the seat and let your manager or client get in second.

....

TIPPING ETIQUETTE

While tipping is discretionary, if you are generous with those who help you, you will be rewarded with better service and a happier heart. And it will reflect well on your company.

Most people know to tip the wait staff 15 to 20 percent of the bill and to give the valet who retrieved your car $2 to $3. In other situations, though, tipping while traveling can be confusing. Here are some of the most common tipping scenarios you'll encounter:

At the Airport

- **Skycaps** are the people who check your bags at the airport curbside and transport them into the terminal. They are not employed by the airlines and rely on tips. The proper amount to tip them is $1 to $2 per bag. Increase the tip if your bag is heavier or larger than usual.

- Pay **taxi and limousine drivers** 15 to 20 percent of the bill.

- Give the rental car or hotel **shuttle driver** $1 per bag.

At the Hotel

- Tip the **doorman** of the hotel $2 for the first bag and $1 for additional bags for taking your luggage out of the car and putting them on the cart. Give him $1 to $3 for getting you a taxi, depending on how difficult it was to hail.

- The **bellman** gets $1 to $2 per bag depending on the size and weight of your bags. If you have a lot of luggage, give him $10 to $12.

- Reward those hardworking **housekeepers** with a tip of $2 to $5 per night. If you ask the housekeeper for special services, such as bringing you an extra pillow or toiletries, leave an additional $1 to $2 in an envelope labeled "Housekeeping" the day you check out. If you stay multiple nights, put the tip on your pillow each day, as the person cleaning your room may change.

- The job of a **concierge** is to suggest restaurants or activities and make reservations. She usually does not expect a tip. However, if she goes above and beyond, such as getting you a reservation to a popular restaurant or securing hard-to-get theater tickets, pay her $5 to $10.

GLOBAL ETIQUETTE

Every country has its cultural norms and ways of communicating in business. When doing business internationally, spend time researching the cultural and communication norms for the country you're visiting. Inadvertently offending your hosts or guests is easy to do if you have not taken the time to understand their cultural nuances.

Understanding a country's context will provide you with a good starting point for making communication and business

ETIQUETTE DILEMMA

Q. *I work for a U.S.-based company that does business globally. We often hold client and vendor meetings in our U.S. offices. Do we need to adhere to the cultural norms of our guests, or should we proceed as if we were doing business with people from the United States?*

A. *If you want to have smooth business dealings, honor the cultural nuances of your guests whether you meet in the United States or in their country. For instance, if rank and authority are important with your client, you'll have more success if your company's highest-ranking person meets with your guest's highest-ranking employee, and you show deference to those with more authority.*

dealings easier. According to anthropologist Edward T. Hall in his book *Beyond Culture*, countries are either high-context or low-context. This is a classification based on how people in different cultures communicate.

High-Context Cultures

High-context countries or regions include Africa, China, France, Greece, India, Indonesia, Japan, South Korea, Spain, Turkey, the Arab world, Latin America and the southern United States. People in high-context cultures emphasize non-verbal communication and rely more on indirect verbal signals. Much is ascertained through nonverbal communication, such as gestures, body language and tone of voice. They also use fewer words, and the words they use can imply other meanings.

Because they are indirect communicators, people from high-context countries, especially Asians, usually don't say "no," which is considered rude. Instead, you might hear phrases like "It's inconvenient," "It's under consideration" or "I'll try." To get a direct answer, ask a question that allows them to say "yes," such as "Do you disagree?"

Time is not a straight-line concept; it has curves and detours. The needs of people may interfere with a timeline. A meeting may be delayed to allow for a meal or to accommodate everyone in the group. Negotiations may slow down to allow for consensus within the group.

People in high-context countries are more formal—rarely calling others by their first names. They also tend to dress more conservatively and modestly—suits or more formal business attire are the norm.

Status and authority are important and valued. Asian cultures, for example, value title and rank and have deep respect for their elders. Decisions are made by the highest-ranking person for the good of the group, and that is emphasized over an individual's ambitions or needs. Rank also dictates things like who enters and exits a room first or last, where people sit and who speaks. It would be insulting to speak to a lower-ranking person before speaking to a person with higher rank, or to seat a high-ranking person from one culture next to someone of lower rank from another culture.

Relationships in high-context cultures are more important than a signed contract; trust is important for forming business relationships.

Low-Context Cultures

On the other end of the scale are the low-context countries—the United States (except for the South), Australia, Canada, New Zealand, Germany, Israel, Switzerland and the Scandinavian countries. In these countries, people rely more on words and less on nonverbal cues to communicate a point. They also tend to use clear and unambiguous wording. No means no and yes means yes.

When it comes to getting things accomplished, time is usually linear. Business moves from point A to point B to point C. Decisions, projects and negotiations have an expected order.

A low-context culture is typically more informal. People tend to dress more casually and are more likely to call others by their first name. Less emphasis is put on rank and title. Decisions can be made by lower-level people within an organization, and formalities, such as seating and who enters or exits first, are not as important.

People from low-context countries are more task-focused than relationship-focused. They are more individualistic and less concerned with the group as a whole. Relationships are important personally, but less so in business.

Because people in low-context cultures value action, clarity and getting down to business, it can be frustrating for them to work with high-context people who are less concerned with timelines and tasks.

I remember speaking to a woman from India who said in the United States we ask others more general questions about where they work and what their job is. When meeting people in India, you will be asked more personal questions about your family, where you grew up and even politics before getting to professional roles.

Countries with the same context can have differences between them as well. Even though Germany and the United States are both low-context countries, we are socially different. I have a German client who describes Americans as peaches. She said we're soft on the outside—friendly and easy to talk to—but we're hard on the inside, like the peach pit; harder to get to know on a deeper level. On the other hand, she described Germans as coconuts: hard on the outside—more formal,

ETIQUETTE DILEMMA

Q. *I am a vegetarian. Is it all right for me to let my foreign hosts know I can't eat meat?*

A. *Yes, you should let your hosts know that because of dietary restrictions or religious beliefs you can't eat meat. However, in some countries, meat is in most dishes and it will be difficult for your hosts to eliminate it. If that's the case, eat what you can and leave the meat.*

brusque and less outwardly friendly. But once you get to know them, they are soft on the inside, and they show this through their warmth and deep friendships.

She told me that when she first came to the United States, she thought Americans were rude because people would ask her personal questions such as how her weekend was or what her vacation plans were. She thought people were being very nosy. Now she understands that these questions are how Americans build rapport and are not meant to be offensive.

Having this knowledge will make your business interactions with people from other cultures smoother. Rather than assuming someone is being difficult, consider their cultural context and norms and how you might respect those customs. Understand, for instance, that if you're interacting with someone from a high-context country, you must build a relationship and earn their trust before you can expect to earn their business.

You'll find many wonderful books with specific information on each country's cultural nuances, tips for doing business and negotiating strategies (a few of them are in the Recommended Reading section). You will have much more success conducting business in other countries when you do your research and become aware of each country's business protocol. You wouldn't want to insult that potential client or business partner.

Have an Open Mind

When traveling to another country, you'll see and experience many differences—how people are greeted, body language, food, eating habits, approach to time, dress and personal space. While your pride in your culture is certainly appropriate, judging your hosts for their cultural differences is counterproductive to both your peace of mind and your business dealings.

When my husband and I were traveling in Italy, we met an

American couple in the Milan train station. We greeted them warmly and were excited to exchange stories about our travel experiences. My husband and I were having a delightful trip and loved the Italian people, the food and the country. We exclaimed, "Isn't this wonderful?!" The husband of the couple had a sour look on his face and replied that he hated every minute and couldn't wait to get home. My husband and I were shocked. We absolutely couldn't understand how anyone could dislike Italy.

Our sense was that he was uncomfortable traveling, and unfortunately his closed mind was keeping him from enjoying the riches before him. Yes, the Italians did things differently. They lingered at their meals, their breakfasts were small, people smoked everywhere even in non smoking trains and noisy scooters were ubiquitous. But rather than being disturbed by the differences, we embraced them and appreciated the dissimilarities. This allowed us to have a very enjoyable trip.

Just Try a Bite

Having an open mind also means trying food and experiences you haven't had before. We tend to get stuck in a rut with our food preferences and routines. The wonderful thing about travel is it gives us an opportunity to break out of our patterns for a time and enjoy new experiences. Maybe you would never eat snails at home, but you might discover escargot is actually a delicious delicacy in France. How would you know if you didn't try it?

When you are served a strange food, be polite by trying a bite or two. If you decide it's not something you enjoy, you don't need to say anything. Simply eat the foods you do like.

When I was fifteen, I traveled to Europe with a nun. My grandmother was a devout Catholic and had planned to take me herself, but as we approached the departure date, she didn't feel strong enough to go. She asked a nun she knew from the church she attended to take me instead. What I thought at age fifteen about traveling with a nun is another story.

We spent the majority of our time in France, but since Sister Maureen had Irish roots, we also spent time exploring Ireland. As we traveled the country, we stayed in farmhouses that included breakfast and dinners in the cost of lodging. The food was always delicious—lots of potatoes and meats with rich gravies. I remember one particular meal included a thick, dark soup. I ate a few spoonfuls and loved it. Curious to know what the soup was, I asked and was told it was oxtail soup. Despite swooning over the deliciousness of this soup moments earlier, suddenly I could no longer stomach it. My mind said "strange,

ETIQUETTE DILEMMA

Q. *We do a lot of business globally. Should we bring gifts to our hosts?*

A. *Gift-giving is an expected tradition in some countries, but not all. In China, Malaysia, Paraguay and Singapore, a gift to an individual can be seen as a bribe, so give a gift that would be appropriate for a group, such as hosting a banquet, especially if you are hosted at one. In other countries including Japan, Indonesia and the Philippines, gift-giving is an important tradition. If that is the case, the wrapping and the presentation of the gift is often just as important as the gift itself. The best gifts are ones that come from the United States. However, avoid knives, scissors, clocks, certain colors and animal-related items such as leather.*

foreign item that you shouldn't like." So, I stopped eating it. Obviously, I did not keep an open mind at that meal, and that was a shame because I missed out on a wonderful soup.

When in Doubt, Ask Your Host

You'll likely encounter food or situations that you aren't sure how to handle, despite your best preparation. When this occurs, watch your host. For example, in Norway use a fork and knife to eat most food, including sandwiches.

You may be served something that seems very challenging to eat. If you can't figure out how to eat it by observing others, go ahead and ask your host. He will appreciate your curiosity and willingness to give things a try, even if you're not quite sure what to do.

CHOPSTICK ETIQUETTE

In countries where chopsticks are present, it is respectful to use them. And you may find many restaurants don't even have forks. This is how to hold them.

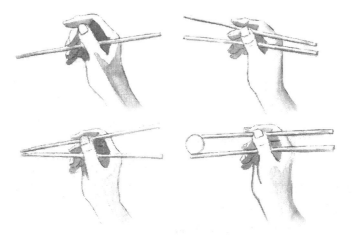

Just as we have silverware etiquette, protocol exists for chopstick use as well. The following rules are important, as you could easily offend others by not adhering to them:

- Don't wave or point your chopsticks at others.
- Never put them sticking up in your rice—which signifies a ritual to honor the dead.
- Don't spear or try to cut food with them (bring the whole piece to your mouth and take a bite).
- Rest your chopsticks on a chopstick stand or on the table with the tips facing to the left, never across your bowl.
- Don't cross your chopsticks when you rest them.
- Avoid licking or chewing on your chopsticks.
- Never rub them together to avoid splinters. This signifies you think the chopsticks are cheap and is insulting to your host.
- Never pass food from person to person by chopsticks. This is symbolic of the passing of the bones of the dead.
- If a serving utensil is not present with the dishes, use the handle end of your chopsticks to take food from the serving dish and put it on your plate.

GESTURE SAVVY

Every country has its unique gestures that are used to communicate a feeling or convey information. For example, we use the thumbs-up motion as a sign of approval. However, this and other common American gestures can get you in hot water when used in other countries. In West Africa, Latin America, Iran, Iraq and Afghanistan, it essentially means "up yours." You can see how easy it would be to offend someone just by using the wrong gesture.

Pay attention to these additional gestures that could be offensive in other countries:

- When Americans want to summon someone, we turn our palm up and use either our pointer finger or all fingers and pull them toward us. However, using a single finger or having an upward palm is considered rude in most other countries. In the Philippines, that is how you call a dog and, if used for a human, could land you in jail. Instead, place your palm down and use a scratching or scooping motion with your fingers.

- The "OK" sign is not okay and is obscene in Russia, Germany and Brazil. In Greece and Turkey, it signifies you're gay.

- Standing or talking to someone with your hands in your pockets is considered rude in many countries.

- Making a fist with your thumb protruding between your middle and index fingers is obscene in some Latin American countries.

- Crossed fingers in the U.S. means you're hoping everything turns out all right, but in Vietnam, it is the sign for a woman's genitals and is basically a vulgar gesture.

- Pointing with one finger is considered bad manners in many countries. If you need to indicate direction or point to something, use all of your fingers. And never point directly at someone; that's offensive in any country.

- In Muslim countries, South Africa and India, the left hand is reserved for cleaning yourself. So, it is considered dirty and would be quite rude to eat or hand someone something with your left hand.

- The "V" sign (for peace or victory in the U.S.) with the back of your hand facing the other person is another obscene gesture in several countries.

- In much of the Far East, especially Malaysia and the Philippines, standing with your hands on your hips is an aggressive posture, as if you're provoking a fight.

- In South Korea, it is respectful to use both hands, or your left hand supporting your right elbow, when handing an item to another person or when receiving something.

Handshakes and Greetings

Besides being a gesture to greet or acknowledge someone, the handshake has great meaning. In the United States, we value a firm handshake because it communicates confidence. We judge someone with a weak handshake as either lacking in confidence or being uninterested. However, the firm, short-held handshake would be seen as presumptuous or arrogant in many East Asian countries.

A WORD ABOUT CHEEK KISSING

The cheek-kiss greeting, where you kiss or touch cheeks, is very common in Latin America, most of Europe, the Mediterranean and the Middle East. However, the practice is typically part of a social interaction and usually takes place only between people who know each other well. Each country and region has different norms. In some countries only women kiss, in others men and women kiss. You'll find that men cheek kiss each other in a few countries.

The number of kisses also depends on the region. For instance, in the South of France expect to do three les bises (touching cheeks and kissing the air). In Paris, the norm is two kisses.[1] When in doubt, start with a handshake and observe your hosts before jumping into a cheek peck.

Take note of the greeting practices of the people with whom you are doing business. Not all people from other countries shake hands, and the handshake differs by country.

Asia: Typically, more westernized Asians or those who do a lot of business with Americans will shake hands. The handshake may be weaker and will usually be held longer.

- If you're in less-populated or less-Westernized areas, a bow is appropriate in Japan.

- In Vietnam, a slight bow with hands clasped above the waist is common.

- A nod of the head with or without a handshake is proper in China and South Korea.

- The gesture called *wai* is the traditional greeting in Thailand. Place your hands together, arms and elbows close to your body, and bow your head to touch your fingers.

- Asian women do not typically shake hands. A western businesswoman will need to initiate a handshake with an Asian man.

Europe: Firm handshakes are usually practiced in Europe. People in some countries, including France and Hungary, will wait for a woman to extend her hand first. French handshakes tend to be softer.

India: Handshakes are typical between men in Westernized areas of India. Women should use the namaste greeting in which one's hands are put together in a prayer position at the chest, head bowed toward your hands, while you say "Namaste" (nuhm-*uh*-stey). For men and women, the namaste greeting is appropriate in less populated, more traditional areas.

Islamic countries: Greetings tend to be complicated; wait for your host to initiate a greeting. Generally, however, Westernized

Muslim men will shake hands with other men. Some men will shake hands with Western women.

Latin America: Shaking hands between men is the usual greeting. In some countries, it may be accompanied with a backslapping embrace called the *abrazo*. Women don't usually shake hands with each other; they typically pat each other on the right arm or shoulder or hug. It's best to wait for a Latina woman to offer her hand before initiating a handshake.

South Africa: Handshakes are common in South Africa between men. Wait for a woman to initiate a handshake before offering yours.

INTERNATIONAL TRAVEL ATTIRE

Business attire in the United States is usually more casual than in most other countries. When doing business outside of the U.S., suits and ties are appropriate for men. For women, a conservative skirt and blouse or pantsuit is proper. Typically, more conservative colors and cuts are appropriate. Skirts and dresses should not be shorter than the knee and blouses should not be revealing in any way. People in many countries value high-quality, well-made clothes and will accord those who wear them more importance.

Business travel has its challenges, but it can be a wonderful way to meet new people and experience interesting places and cultures. Keep an open mind and be courteous and gracious so that you represent yourself and your company well. You and those with whom you interact will enjoy the experience much more.

SOME PARTING WORDS

I sometimes get out my copy of Amy Vanderbilt's *Everyday Etiquette* to see how much etiquette has changed since the book was written in the 1950s. There I find sections on when a man should remove his hat, and on the placement of a secretary's steno dictation pad when transcribing a letter for her boss. While most men don't wear formal hats today, secretaries are now executive assistants, and dictation has been replaced by email, these scenarios were about respect—and respect is still important for a profitable, happy workplace.

When you are respectful, courteous and kind and conduct yourself professionally, you will prosper. It takes time to learn new skills—usually about ninety days of practicing what you've learned. Just reading this book will not imbue you with perfect etiquette and manners. I encourage you to practice one new skill that you've learned from the book each week. Whether you focus on the etiquette of conducting a meeting, dining with your boss or making business introductions—eventually you'll know what to do without thinking. And when you reach that place of knowing, you'll be more confident, relaxed and successful in most business situations.

To your success!

There is no accomplishment so easy to acquire as politeness, and none more profitable.

—H.W. Shaw

ACKNOWLEDGMENTS

We can only be said to be alive in those moments
when our hearts are conscious of our treasures.

—Thornton Wilder

I am so grateful and deeply indebted to the many people who encouraged me, pushed me, advised me and challenged me through this book publishing journey. The book could not have come to fruition had it not been for your support. I treasure you all.

Maria Everding, my etiquette instructor, friend and mentor. You didn't tell me to get lost when I had so many newbie etiquette and business questions. Your patience and support helped me to turn a passion into a thriving business. And your anecdotes live on in my trainings and coaching sessions—"Unless you're waiting for a kidney, never answer your phone in the presence of others."

Carole Cancler, your willingness to meet for regular writing dates (and happily eat doughnuts too), helped me to finish the book. And while maddening at times, your oh-so-wise and direct feedback on the manuscript made it more inclusive and relatable. Thank you for always being there for me.

I so appreciate my other wonderful manuscript readers: my dad, John Clise, and friends Catherine Pages, Janet Sittig and Ruth Woods. You each shared unique views on the content which was invaluable in strengthening the book.

An introvert shout-out to Beth Buelow, my friend and former

business-accountability partner. You were my inspiration and quiet cheerleader as I wrote this book over four years. Watching your impressive publishing accomplishments pushed me to keep going.

Shari Storm, you were one of my first friends who had written a book. Our meeting many years ago to discuss your publishing path was the initial step in my decision to write this book. Your friendship and support over the years has meant so much to me.

To my publisher and friend, Peg Markworth, and her assistant, Julia Ogburn, with Silver Fern Publishing. Thank you for taking me under your wing and advising, supporting and encouraging me. You are gifts!

Much gratitude goes to Mimi Kirsch, who wrote the beautiful foreword. I feel so honored you took the time to share your thoughts about my book.

Cheers to friends Posy Gering, Laura Leist and Marschel Paul. You offered advice, resources and encouragement that kept me moving forward with this book.

Thank you to my many clients, colleagues, friends and newsletter and blog readers. Your stories and questions provided much fodder and structure for the book. Much appreciation also to my Facebook friends who offered book-related advice and opinions.

And to my beloved husband, Eric Mamroth, chief cook and bottle-washer, who kept me from starving while I worked on this book. Six years ago, you encouraged me to quit my job and start my business even though it was scary for both of us. Thank you for allowing me to follow my passion and for being my go-to, dependable guy on this fun and wild ride.

RECOMMENDED READING

Books

Baldrige, Letitia. *Letitia Baldrige's Complete Guide to the New Manners for the '90s: A Complete Guide To Etiquette*. New York, NY: Scribner, 2014.

Buelow, Beth L. *The Introvert Entrepreneur: Amplify Your Strengths and Create Success on Your Own Terms*. New York, NY: Perigee Books, 2015.

Carnegie, Dale. *How to Win Friends and Influence People*. New York, NY: Pocket Books, 1998.

Everding, Maria Perniciaro. *Panache That Pays: The Young Professional's Guide: How to Outclass Your Competition*. St. Louis, MO: GME, 1997.

Hessler, Jim, and Steve Motenko. *Land on Your Feet, Not on Your Face: A Guide to Building Your Leadership Platform*. Seattle, WA: Bennett & Hastings, 2010.

Hickey, Robert. *Honor and Respect: The Official Guide to Names, Titles, and Forms of Address*. Washington, DC: Protocol School of Washington, 2014.

Howell, Lorraine. *Give Your Elevator Speech a Lift!* Bothell, WA: Book Network, 2006.

Manciagli, Dana. *Cut the Crap, Get a Job! A New Job Search Process for a New Era*. Gold River, CA: Authority, 2013.

McKay, Brett, and Kate McKay. *The Art of Manliness: Classic Skills and Manners for the Modern Man*. Cincinnati, OH: HOW, 2009.

Mitchell, Mary. *The Complete Idiot's Guide to Etiquette.* New York, NY: Alpha, 1996.

Morrison, Terri, Wayne A. Conaway, and George A. Borden. *Kiss, Bow, or Shake Hands: How to Do Business in Sixty Countries.* Holbrook, MA: B. Adams, 1994.

Rickenbacher, Colleen A. *Be on Your Best Cultural Behavior: How to Avoid Social and Professional Faux Pas When Dining, Traveling, Conversing, and Entertaining.* United States: Colleen A. Rickenbacher, 2008.

Rosemont, Debbie. *Six Word Lessons to Be More Productive.* Sammamish, WA: Leading on the Edge International, 2009.

Sandberg, Sheryl, and Nell Scovell. *Lean In: Women, Work, and the Will to Lead.* New York, NY: Knopf, 2013.

Shepherd, Margaret. *The Art of the Handwritten Note: A Guide to Reclaiming Civilized Communications.* New York, NY: Broadway, 2002.

Sittig-Rolf, Andrea. *Power Referrals: The Ambassador Method for Empowering Others to Promote Your Business and Do the Selling for You.* New York, NY: McGraw-Hill, 2009.

Storm, Shari. *Motherhood Is the New MBA: Using Your Parenting Skills to Be a Better Boss.* New York, NY: Thomas Dunne, 2009.

von Drachenfels, Suzanne. *The Art of the Table: A Complete Guide to Table Setting, Table Manners, and Tableware.* New York, NY: Simon & Schuster, 2000.

Whitmore, Jacqueline. *Business Class: Etiquette Essentials for Success at Work.* New York, NY: St. Martin's, 2005.

Websites and Internet Resources

Fine Stationery
www.finestationery.com

The Introvert Entrepreneur Podcast
www.itunes.apple.com/us/podcast/the-introvert
-entrepreneur/id387593948

Recognition Works
www.recognitionworks.net

Toastmasters International
www.toastmasters.org

NOTES

Introduction

1. Giblin, James Cross. *From Hand to Mouth, Or, How We Invented Knives, Forks, Spoons, and Chopsticks, and the Table Manners to Go with Them.* New York, NY: Crowell, 1987.

Chapter One
Handshake or Fist Bump? Presenting Your Best Self

1. Sandberg, Sheryl. *Lean In: Women, Work, and the Will to Lead.* New York, NY: Knopf, 2013.

2. Goman, Carol Kinsey, "Great Leaders Talk with Their Hands." Forbes.com, September 21, 2010. http://www.forbes.com/2010/09/21/body-language-hands-gestures-forbes-woman-leadership-communication.html.

3. "Swearing at Work Can Harm Your Career Prospects, Finds CareerBuilder Survey." Careerbuilder.com, July 25, 2012. http://www.careerbuilder.com/share/aboutus/pressreleasesdetail.aspx?sd=7%2F25%2F2012&sc_cmp1=cb_pr709_&siteid=cbpr&id=pr709&ed=12%2F31%2F2012.

Chapter Three
Hello, My Name Is Jane:
Meeting and Mingling with Ease

1. "Which Is Worse: Networking or Dating?" *Seattle Times,* December 4, 2014.

Chapter Seven
Yikes! My Boss Sent Me a Friend Request: Digital Diplomacy

1. *The U.S. Digital Consumer Report.* Nielsen, February 10, 2014. http://www.nielsen.com/us/en/insights/reports/2014/the-us-digital-consumer-report.html.

2. Heggestuen, John. "One in Every 5 People in the World Own a Smartphone, One in Every 17 Own a Tablet" *Business Insider,* December 15, 2013. http://www.businessinsider.com/smartphone-and-tablet-penetration-2013-10.

3. Smith, Aaron. "U.S. Smartphone Use in 2015." *Pew Research Center,* April 1, 2015. http://www.pewinternet.org/2015/04/01/us-smartphone-use-in-2015/?beta=true&utm_expid=53098246-2.Lly4CFSVQG2lphsg-KopIg.1&utm_referrer=https%3A%2F%2Fwww.google.com.

4. Facebook Newsroom. http://newsroom.fb.com/company-info/.

Chapter Eight
Two Kisses or One? Travel Etiquette in a Global World

1. Opaz, Gabriella. "To Kiss or Not to Kiss: Top 10 Tips for Greeting Fellow Europeans." Catavino.net, July 5, 2010. http://catavino.net/to-kiss-or-not-to-kiss-top-10-tips-for-greeting-fellow-europeans/.

Morrison, Terri, Wayne A. Conaway, and George A. Borden. *Kiss, Bow, or Shake Hands: How to Do Business in Sixty Countries.* Holbrook, MA: B. Adams, 1994.

Rickenbacher, Colleen A. *Be on Your Best Cultural Behavior: How to Avoid Social and Professional Faux Pas When Dining,*

Traveling, Conversing, and Entertaining. United States: Colleen A. Rickenbacher, 2008.

INDEX

ABOUT THE AUTHOR

Arden Clise is founder of Clise Etiquette, a company that offers contemporary business etiquette, communications and customer service seminars. Arden's love for business etiquette began in  previous jobs when she was frequently asked for etiquette, public speaking and business attire advice by executives and board members. The passion for etiquette took hold and compelled Arden to start a consulting business to help others. Today, as a professional trainer, coach and speaker, Arden has helped thousands of professionals, from executives to front line staff, confidently and comfortably navigate business situations for career success.

A popular writer, Arden has written a regular business etiquette column for the *Puget Sound Business Journal,* and currently writes an award-winning newsletter. She is often quoted in national and international publications including *Real Simple* magazine, the *Wall Street Journal* and *China Daily USA,* and is a frequent guest on radio and television shows.

Arden received her certification as an etiquette consultant from The Etiquette Institute and earned her bachelor's degree in English literature from the University of Washington.

A Seattle native, Arden lives with her husband, Eric Mamroth, their assorted menagerie of foster and resident dogs, and one unhappy cat.

For more information about Arden Clise and Clise Etiquette visit www.cliseetiquette.com.

Made in the USA
Lexington, KY
14 January 2017